Hazel's
Kitchen Table

Pull up a chair, enjoy home-cooked recipes and memories of a time gone by.

by Jeanne Larson Hyde

Library of Congress Catalog Card Number: 97-092883

Published by
JeannieBean
Wisconsin Rapids, Wisconsin 54494

Printed in the United States of America by
Palmer Publications, Inc.
318 North Main Street
PO Box 296
Amherst, Wisconsin 54406

Designed and marketed by
Amherst Press
A division of Palmer Publications, Inc.
PO Box 296
Amherst, Wisconsin 54406

Dedication

This book is dedicated to the future generations:

Alexis and Alison Hyde

Katie and Eric Mandelin

Gavin Smiley

May the past be important to their futures.

Bernice and Hazel.

Contents

Acknowledgments

Thank you to everyone who took the time to share their stories and memories with me. Your help was immeasurable and very enjoyable.

A special thanks and a big hug to my husband Mike whose patience, creativity and computer skills were vital. I couldn't have done it without you!

Introduction

Above all else there was the laughter. One could not sit at Hazel Larson's kitchen table without laughing. In these days of formal dining rooms and kitchen counters with stools, it seems sadly nostalgic remembering a kitchen table as a meeting place. Hazel's kitchen was anything but formal, and more was served than just food.

Beginning in the 1930s, Hazel's special brand of friendship and humor attracted people who kept returning for years and years just to sit at her table. It was a place to share a cup of coffee, pastry and conversation. Through the years the chairs at that table have been filled with many people with diverse backgrounds. From immigrant cherry pickers to doctors and lawyers, everyone was treated as though they were family. The ever present cup of coffee was enjoyed by all.

Some Saturday mornings, but never before 9:00 a.m. please!, Hazel's kitchen would get so crowded that it would be standing room only. Twenty conversations would be going on at the same time, but somehow Hazel remained the center of attention. She never missed greeting someone or bidding them farewell. She merely kept refilling the coffee pot and saying "help yourself." Of course with the coffee was always something to tempt the taste buds, and whether it was cake, pie, cookies or pastry, it was always homemade.

Appropriately enough, my mother, Bernice Larson, first met her new sister-in-law Hazel (their husbands were twins) at that table. Arriving by way of Duluth and Chicago, my mom was taught the ways of "country life" by Hazel. They soon would become close friends, and that friendship would last a lifetime. They were both "stubborn Swedes," enjoyed cooking, laughed a lot and were very caring. And they both had kitchen tables.

It was in Hazel's kitchen that the idea for this cookbook was conceived. The evening before Hazel's funeral, the family was gathered around her kitchen table (surprise!). The mood was somber at first because everyone knew that it wasn't the table that was special, but the people missing from it. And we remembered the laughter. My mom's laugh came from deep within. It filled the whole room and was truly joyful. Hazel's laughter was usually punctuated with a loud "ha!" and was contagious. The conversation then turned to all the wonderful food Hazel and my mom had prepared through the years. It seemed most of our memories were centered around their cooking. Family and friends alike have memories to be cherished for a lifetime.

It was then I realized I had to do more than record recipes. Each one of these recipes contains a piece of our lives.

+>>> ✳ <<<+

Aunt Hazel—The Country Girl

Hazel in 1960.

Emil and Hulda Elquist raised six children in a large home in Ellison Bay near what is now Newport State Park in Door County, Wisconsin. Their youngest, Hazel, became the most adventuresome of the family. The thrill of travel and her independent nature lured her, at 16 years of age, to Chicago where she worked as a housekeeper. She returned home in the summers to work as a waitress at a local resort.

Hazel eventually settled down, married Everett Larson (my father's twin brother) and moved to Appleport in 1933. She quickly became an integral part of the Larson family and worked in their lucrative fishing and cherry orchard businesses. She could nail together fish boxes and operate the spray rig at the orchard with the best of them.

Hazel's personal qualities resulted in making her a true Door County "character." She was fiercely independent, a colorful story teller with a wonderful sense of humor, and her love of life was always evident. It was also these traits that carried her through life's misfortunes: her husband's tragic death in 1956 and the loss of her only son in 1987 were terrible blows to her. She carried on because she refused to feel sorry for herself. She was always more interested in the well-being of others. After Hazel's children (Wink and Betty) left home, the lure of travel and a warmer climate took her to Florida and California in the winters. "As long as my feet can carry me, I'm going with them."

Hazel led a full life and tried to keep it simple. Modern conveniences weren't important. She continued to use the same wringer washer she had acquired in the 1940s. Auctions, garage sales, playing cards, and of course, bingo were her great passions. She would purchase boxes of items "for cheap" at auctions and resell them at a small profit at her own perpetual garage sale. Tending her garden was another source of satisfaction. Many hours were spent planting, weeding, watering and finding new and inventive ways to fend off deer and rabbit invasions.

Hazel still wringing.

Hazel's health prevented her from going away the last few winters, but everyone enjoyed her company and hearing the coffee pot perking the year-round. Even though health problems caused her much discomfort and hampered her ability to do the things she enjoyed, she never complained. If you asked her how she felt, she merely responded "not so good," and the subject was quickly changed. It is funny, however, her feet couldn't travel the way they used to, but they never got any lighter on the gas pedal.

In the fall of 1995, Hazel passed away at the age of 84 as a result of injuries sustained in a fall. I lost more than an aunt. I lost a confidant, a friend and a second mother. Her optimism, inner strength, laughter and love will be never be forgotten by her family and friends. Hazel blessed many people in many ways and our lives, although enriched because of her, will not be the same without her. "If you don't learn to have fun and laugh a little, you're in trouble," she once said. "Me, I get a kick out of just being alive."

My Mom—The City Girl

In addition to her laughter, my mom is most remembered for her remarkable patience. Growing up in the harsh, cold winters of Duluth, Minnesota, may have taught her these values. You had to be patient waiting for spring to arrive in Duluth. I'm certain her upbringing in a Swedish household also contributed.

Born Bernice Sandberg, she attended Denfeld High School in Duluth's "West End." She excelled in school, particularly the home economic classes that were to form the basis for her cooking skills. Her love of cooking was evident and continued throughout her life. While growing up, she loved to visit her grandparents' farm in Port Wing, Wisconsin. She spent many summers there with her brother Clarence and sister Bertha. It was also in Port Wing (at the Wigwam Dance Hall) where she first met her future husband, Emery Larson, a commercial fisherman. After a brief courtship, they were married in Chicago where Emery, my father, was stationed in the Coast Guard during World War II. Fortunately the war ended the day my dad was scheduled to be shipped overseas.

After the war he packed up his family, which now included sons John and Richard, and moved to Door County (his birthplace). He got a job tending a cherry orchard and also helping with the family fishing business. They rented a house in Ellison Bay that much to my mother's dismay had no indoor plumbing.

With granddaughter Alison.

With granddaughter Lexie.

It was quite a shock for a city girl! She persevered, however, and shortly thereafter they bought a home in Appleport just outside of Sister Bay. It was here that her great love for country living began, and in the late '40s and '50s, she was involved in every aspect of it—helping in the fishing business and cherry orchard, bringing up a family (that now included me!) and doing it all with laughter and love.

Even though country life moves at a slower pace, time passes quickly. Soon the children were grown and in 1975 my dad died. She carried on and never lost her positive outlook on life; it was just moving in a different direction. She waited patiently for something that would enrich her life—grandchildren. Finally in the early '80s, two granddaughters arrived, and they soon became the light of her life.

In 1984 my mom had a close call but survived open heart surgery. Every year after that was referred to as a "bonus year." She spent those years spoiling her grandchildren, and as most grandparents do, she spoke endlessly and proudly of them. Cancer finally claimed her life in 1990, but her laughter, optimism and love lasted to the very end. She is missed by all.

Baked Goods

Danish Pastry

These pastries look very elegant but are surprisingly simple to make. The secret to a flaky pastry is to layer the dough by rolling and folding.

Yield: 5 dozen rolls

2 cups lukewarm water
1/2 cup sugar
1 cake (2 ounces) yeast
1 tablespoon salt
6 1/2 cups flour, sifted, divided
2 eggs
1/3 cup shortening, melted and cooled
1 cup butter, divided

Frosting:
1/2 cup powdered sugar
2 tablespoons half-and-half
1/2 teaspoon vanilla extract

Combine water, sugar and yeast in a large mixing bowl. Add salt and 2 cups of the sifted flour. Beat with electric mixer on medium speed for 2 minutes.

Add eggs and shortening; beat 1 minute. Gradually add remaining 4 1/2 cups flour, stirring until dough is formed. For ease in handling, allow dough to rest in bowl for 20 minutes at room temperature.

Roll dough into a 15x18-inch rectangle on a floured board. Cut 1/2 cup of the butter into thin slices and place on center 1/3 of the rectangle. Fold the right unbuttered portion onto the buttered portion and seal edges with heel of hand.

Slice remaining 1/2 cup butter and place on the double portion of dough. Fold the left unbuttered portion onto the buttered portion and seal edges with heel of hand.

(continued)

Roll dough again into a 15x18-inch rectangle. Fold right 1/3 of rectangle onto the center 1/3 portion, then fold left 1/3 of dough onto center portion. Repeat rolling and folding process twice. Cover with plastic wrap and refrigerate at least 30 minutes.

On a lightly floured board, roll dough into a rectangle 1/8 inch thick. Cut dough into strips 1/2 inches by 8 inches long; twist each strip. Holding one end of twisted strip, swirl the remainder of strip around center.

Spray 4 cookie sheets with nonstick cooking spray. Place rolls on sheets in rows about 2 inches apart. Cover rolls with a clean towel and let rise in a warm place, approximately 40 minutes.

Preheat oven to 375 degrees. Bake rolls for 18-20 minutes or until golden brown. Remove from oven; cool on wire rack.

To make frosting, in a small bowl, blend powdered sugar, cream and vanilla. Mix until smooth. Frost cooled rolls.

Note: Dough may be stored in the refrigerator for 2 or 3 days when carefully wrapped.

When we would ask Hazel how to cook or bake something, she would say there was nothing to it: "you know, a cup of this or a pinch of that."

—Barb and Nel
(regulars at Hazel's
kitchen table)

Swedish Limpa

*This is the premier bread baked
in the Swedish kitchen.*

Yield: 2 round loaves

1 package (1/4 ounce) dry yeast
1 cup plus 2 tablespoons lukewarm water
1 cup milk, scalded
1/4 cup shortening
2 tablespoons caraway seeds
1 tablespoon salt
1/4 cup molasses
3 cups rye flour
1 tablespoon grated orange rind
3 1/2 cups white flour

In a small bowl, dissolve yeast in 2 tablespoons of the water.

Combine milk, shortening, caraway seeds, salt, molasses and remaining 1 cup water in a large bowl; cool to lukewarm. Add yeast, rye flour and orange rind; beat well. Stir in as much of the white flour as you can or until the dough is slightly sticky. Turn onto a floured board. Let rest 10 minutes.

Knead dough about 5-10 minutes, adding more flour as needed. (The dough will be smooth and elastic in appearance.) Place in a greased bowl, turning once to grease other side. Cover with clean, dry towel and let rise until doubled in size, about 1 hour.

When dough has doubled, punch down and return to floured board. Divide in half and shape into round loaves. Place on 2 cookie sheets which have been sprayed with non-stick cooking spray. Cut 2 small slits in top of each loaf. Cover with a dry towel and let rise again, about 30 minutes.

While Appleport has no formal boundaries, my dad always used to joke that we lived "on the elite side of the dump."

(continued)

Preheat oven to 400 degrees. Bake 10 minutes; reduce heat to 375 degrees and continue baking for 40 minutes. Remove from pans and let cool on wire rack. Make sure bread is completely cool before slicing.

Apricot Cranberry Bread

Apricots and cranberries may seem an unusual combination, but I guarantee that you will be baking this bread more than once.

Yield: 2 small loaves

2 cups flour
3/4 cup sugar
1 tablespoon baking powder
1/2 teaspoon salt
2 eggs, beaten
1 cup milk
1/4 cup butter, melted
1 cup chopped dried apricots
1 cup chopped fresh cranberries
1/2 cup nuts, chopped
1 teaspoon grated orange rind

Preheat oven to 350 degrees. Spray 2 small bread pans with nonstick cooking spray.

Sift flour, sugar, baking powder and salt together into a large bowl. Add eggs, milk and butter; mix well. Stir in apricots, cranberries, nuts and orange rind.

Divide batter in half and place into prepared pans. Bake 60 minutes. Remove from oven and cool 10 minutes in pans. Remove from pans and place on wire racks to cool.

Lexie's Pancakes

Very good! That is the description my mom had beside this recipe. She may have been a little prejudiced since Lexie was her granddaughter and was about six years old at the time. This is the exact recipe.

Yield: 4-6 pancakes

1 cup or scoop flour
1 cup sugar
1 egg
1 cup milk
1 teaspoon baking powder
1 teaspoon oil

Let sit about 3 hours or 1 minute. Then you fry them on a frying pan.

Swedish Pancakes
(Plattar)

An end to a great weekend was the arrival of Swedish Pancakes hot off the griddle. They were the traditional send-off. You knew you were really somebody if they were prepared just for you. Of course they can be served at any time of day. "They are not just for breakfast anymore." The trick is to prepare the batter several hours ahead of time or the night before.

Yield: 12 to 15 pancakes

1 cup milk
1 cup water
4 eggs
1 teaspoon salt
1/4 cup sugar
2 cups sifted flour
4 tablespoons butter, melted

Combine milk, water, eggs, salt, sugar, flour and butter in blender; blend 1 minute. Store covered in refrigerator several hours or overnight.

Preheat griddle that has been lightly sprayed with nonstick cooking spray. Pour and spread batter into thin 4-6 inch round cakes. Fry 1-2 minutes or until lightly browned. Carefully turn over and repeat.

Serve with syrup or fresh fruit.

My Grandma Hazel was very special. She was more than just a grandmother to me, she was my best friend, and I could talk to her about anything. As a kid growing up, I remember she made the most delicious Swedish pancakes. The on-going joke was between Grandma and Al Johnson, and who made the better pancakes. I always worked this to my advantage, and depending on whose table I was at, those were the best! (For the record, she made the best.)

—Mitch Larson
(Hazel's grandson)

Butterhorns

Church bazaars and bake sales on a cool, crisp autumn day conjure up an image of women setting out freshly baked, homemade goodies on a long covered table. Of course butterhorns were there in great plenty— but not for long.

Yield: 2$\frac{1}{2}$ dozen butterhorns

    1 cup milk, scalded
    1 cake (2 ounces) yeast
    4 cups flour
$\frac{1}{2}$ cup granulated sugar
    1 teaspoon salt
$\frac{3}{4}$ cup shortening
    2 eggs, slightly beaten
1$\frac{1}{2}$ cups brown sugar
$\frac{1}{2}$ cup nuts, crushed
    2 cups powdered sugar
    4 teaspoons water

Cool milk to lukewarm. Add yeast and stir until dissolved.

Sift flour, granulated sugar and salt into a large bowl. Cut in shortening until it resembles the size of small peas. Stir in yeast mixture and eggs. Cover dough with a towel and let stand overnight.

Spray 3 cookie sheets with nonstick cooking spray.

In a small bowl, mix together brown sugar and nuts; set aside. Divide dough into 4 parts. Roll each part like pie crust and cut into 8 pie-shaped wedges. Place 1 teaspoon of sugar and nut mixture near wide end of each wedge and roll to center. Repeat process. Place on cookie sheet. Cover with a towel and let rise until doubled, about 45 minutes.

(continued)

Preheat oven to 350 degrees. While oven is preheating, mix together powdered sugar and water. Add enough water until mixture is slightly thick.

Bake butterhorns 7-8 minutes. Remove from oven and place on wire rack. Frost hot butterhorns with powdered sugar frosting.

Good for Dunkin' Donuts

These donuts require nothing more than to be savored
for breakfast or with your morning coffee break.
My mom treated her guests to these many, many times.

Yield: 3 to 4 dozen donuts

4 cups flour
4 teaspoons baking powder
1/2 teaspoon salt
1/4 teaspoon nutmeg
2 eggs, beaten
1 cup sugar
2 tablespoons butter, melted
1 cup milk
1/4 teaspoon lemon extract
3 cups cooking oil

Sift together flour, baking powder, salt and nutmeg in a large bowl. Add eggs, sugar, butter, milk and lemon extract; mix well. Place dough on a lightly floured board and roll to a thickness of 1/2 inch. Cut donuts with donut cutter and place on plain waxed paper. Save several donut holes for frying too.

Heat oil to 185 degrees (on a candy thermometer) in a medium saucepan. Fry donuts 1-2 minutes; turning to brown each side evenly. Remove from pan; set on paper towel to cool and remove excess oil. Store in tightly covered container.

Bernice's Biscuits

*Any special meal required my mom's biscuits
"from scratch." She seemed to make them so effortlessly.
The image of her kneading the dough at the kitchen
counter is such a warm, rich memory.*

Yield: 4 dozen biscuits

  1 cake (2 ounces) yeast
1 1/2 cups lukewarm water, divided
  1 cup milk, scalded
1/4 cup shortening
1/2 cup sugar
  3 teaspoons salt
  2 eggs, slightly beaten
  8 cups sifted flour, divided

In a small bowl, dissolve yeast into 1/2 cup of the water.

Combine milk, remaining 1 cup water, shortening, sugar and salt in a large bowl. Cool to lukewarm. Add eggs. Gradually stir in 4 cups of the flour until batter is slightly thick; beat well. Add remaining 4 cups flour and stir until dough is thick and leaves sides of bowl. Turn onto a floured board. Knead 5-10 minutes, adding just enough flour to keep it from sticking to the board. Shape into a ball and place in a greased bowl. Turn over to grease both sides of ball. Cover with a clean towel and set in a warm place to rise, about 1 1/2 hours.

When dough is doubled in size, punch down and return to floured board. Let rest 10 minutes.

Spray two 13x9-inch cake pans with nonstick cooking spray. Break off small pieces of dough and shape into balls. Place 1 inch apart in prepared pans. Cover and let rise 30 minutes or until doubled in size.

(continued)

A guest never forgets the host who has treated him kindly.

—Homer

Preheat oven to 375 degrees. Bake 15 minutes or until browned and hollow sounding when tapped. Remove from pans and cool on wire rack. While biscuits are still warm, brush tops with shortening for a softer crust.

Date Bread

This is a great bread to have in your freezer when those unexpected guests come knocking at your door. Add some cream cheese and enjoy!

Yield: 2 small loaves

1 cup boiling water
1 cup dates, chopped
6 tablespoons shortening
1 cup sugar
1 egg
1 teaspoon vanilla extract
1 1/2 cups flour
1 teaspoon baking soda
1 cup nuts, chopped

Preheat oven to 375 degrees. Spray 2 small loaf pans with nonstick cooking spray.

In a small bowl, combine water and dates; set aside.

Combine shortening, sugar, egg and vanilla in a large bowl; mix well. Stir in date mixture. Sift flour and baking soda together; add to mixture. Blend until batter is moist; stir in nuts.

Pour into prepared pans. Bake 40-45 minutes. Cool in pans 10 minutes. Remove from pans and finish cooling on a wire rack.

Stollen

A wonderful Swedish bread generally made at Christmas. It is colorful, moist and very tasty.

Yield: 1 stollen

1 package (1/4 ounce) dry yeast
1/4 cup lukewarm water
3/4 cup milk, scalded and cooled
    to lukewarm
2 1/2 cups flour, divided
1/4 cup butter, melted
3/4 teaspoon salt
1 tablespoon sugar
3/4 cup candied fruit, cut up
1/4 cup raisins

Soften yeast in warm water in a large bowl. Add milk and 1 1/4 cups of the flour; mix well. Cover and let rise in a warm place until doubled in size, about 1 hour.

Add butter, salt, sugar, fruit, raisins and remaining 1 1/4 cups flour; mix until well blended. Turn dough onto a lightly floured board and knead until smooth and satiny, about 5-8 minutes. Place in a greased bowl, cover and let rise in a warm place again until doubled. Punch down and place on a lightly floured board. Flatten, cover and let rest 10 minutes.

Roll into a 1-inch-thick circle. Crease circle to one side of center. Brush larger side with butter. Fold smaller side over larger side. Place on cookie sheet which has been prepared with nonstick cooking spray. Brush top with butter, cover and let rise in a warm place until doubled.

Preheat oven to 375 degrees. Bake 35 minutes. Remove and place on wire rack to cool, about 5 minutes. Frost with Powdered Sugar Frosting.

Powdered Sugar Frosting

Yield: 1 cup

1 tablespoon boiling water
1 teaspoon lemon juice
3/4 cup powdered sugar, sifted

To make frosting, add boiling water and lemon juice to sugar in a small bowl. Mix thoroughly. Spread evenly on top of cooled stollen.

Baking Powder Biscuits

What an addition piping hot biscuits make to a meal! My dad always claimed he could make them the best, but he was never willing to prove it to us. Hence this is not his recipe.

Yield: 15 biscuits

2 cups flour
4 teaspoons baking powder
1/2 teaspoon salt
1/4 cup shortening
3/4 cup milk

Preheat oven to 425 degrees. Spray a cookie sheet with nonstick cooking spray.

Sift flour, baking powder and salt into a medium bowl. With a pastry blender or fork, cut shortening into dry ingredients until mixture looks like coarse meal. Add milk, stirring just until moistened. Turn dough onto a floured board.

Knead dough about 30 seconds. Pat to a thickness of 1/2 inch; cut with a floured round cookie cutter. Place on prepared sheet. Bake 15 minutes or until golden brown.

Grammy's White Bread

My mom was known for baking the best bread in Appleport and beyond. Perhaps it was because she made it so often, but I suspect it was the love and patience she put into all her baking. There is no aroma that can make me homesick more quickly than this bread baking in the oven.

Yield: 2 loaves

1 cake (2 ounces) yeast
1 1/4 cups lukewarm water, divided
1 cup milk, scalded
2 tablespoons sugar
2 teaspoons salt
6 cups sifted flour, divided
1 tablespoon shortening

Crumble yeast into 1/4 cup of the water; soften 5 minutes.

Pour milk into a large mixing bowl; add sugar, salt and remaining 1 cup water. Stir until sugar and salt are dissolved; cool until lukewarm.

Pour softened yeast into milk mixture. Stir until yeast is well blended. Add 1/2 of the sifted flour to milk mixture. Stir until dough is thoroughly mixed.

Melt shortening; allow to cool. Add to dough. Add remaining flour and mix well. Stir until dough comes away from sides of bowl. Turn onto a floured board and let rest 10 minutes. Knead 10-12 minutes. Shape into a smooth ball and place in a large greased bowl. Turn dough in bowl to grease entire surface. Cover with a clean, dry towel and set in a warm place. Allow dough to rise (approximately 2 hours) or until doubled in size. When dough has doubled, punch down and turn over. Cover and allow to double again, about 1 hour.

(continued)

Spray two 9x5x3-inch loaf pans with nonstick cooking spray. Punch dough down again and turn onto a floured board. Divide dough in half, shape into loaves and place in loaf pans. Cover loaf pans with a dry towel and let rise in a warm place until doubled in size, about 1 hour.

Preheat oven to 400 degrees. Bake loaves approximately 50 minutes or until crust is light brown and bread has a hollow sound when top is tapped. Remove from pans and cool on wire racks.

Note: For a softer crust, brush top with melted shortening.

When it came to baking bread, my mom was the best. One summer there was a great mystery surrounding the bread in the bread box—it kept disappearing! Finally after weeks of wonder, my mom discovered why we were raising the fattest, happiest chickens around. From then on, there was a dent in the cover of that old tin bread box to prevent my 3-year-old hands from opening it.

Raised Donuts

*Fresh out of the fryer and dipped in sugar, these donuts
will melt in your mouth. Add a cup of hot coffee,
and you won't be able to keep the neighbors away.
These donuts freeze well too.*

Yield: 2 dozen donuts

1 1/4 cups milk, divided
1 cake (2 ounces) yeast
1/2 cup shortening
4 1/2 cups flour
1/2 cup sugar
3 eggs, beaten
1 lemon rind, grated
3 cups vegetable oil

Scald 1 cup of the milk in a small saucepan; set aside to cool. Dissolve yeast in remaining 1/4 cup milk.

Using a pastry blender or fork, cut shortening into flour and sugar until mixture resembles the size of small peas. Add milk-yeast mixture, eggs and lemon rind; blend well.

Put dough in a clean oiled bowl and cover with a towel. Set in a warm place and let rise until doubled in size, about 1 hour. When doubled, punch down and place on a floured board. Roll dough to a thickness of 1/2 inch. Cut donuts with donut cutter and place on plain waxed paper. Let rise until doubled again, about 30 minutes.

Heat oil to 185 degrees in a medium saucepan (use a candy thermometer). Fry donuts 3 or 4 at a time, about 1 1/2 minutes; turning to brown each side evenly. Set on a cookie sheet lined with paper towels and cool. Roll donuts in sugar when thoroughly cooled.

Casseroles and
Side Dishes

Cucumbers and Vinegar

Tending their gardens took up a good deal of time in the summer. This recipe was mandatory after picking the first cucumbers of the season.

Yield: 4 servings

2-3 larger cucumbers, peeled and sliced thin
1 small onion, sliced
2 teaspoons salt
2 cups water
2/3 cup vinegar
6 tablespoons sugar
1/2 teaspoon black pepper

Combine cucumbers, onion and salt in a medium bowl; cover completely with water. Let stand 1 hour.

Drain and return cucumbers to bowl; add vinegar, sugar and pepper. Stir until sugar is dissolved.

Refrigerate at least 3 hours before serving.

I made me gardens and orchards, and I planted trees in them of all kinds of fruit.

—Ecclesiastes 2:5

Sour Cream Cucumbers

Summertime signals the advent of fresh cucumbers either from your garden or a farmers' market. Combining with sour cream makes them irresistible.

Yield: 4-6 servings

5 medium cucumbers,
  peeled and sliced thin
1 1/2 tablespoons salt, divided
2 cups cold water
1 carton (8 ounces) sour cream
3 tablespoons wine vinegar
1 tablespoon sugar
1 small onion, cut in eighths
1/2 teaspoon black pepper

Mix cucumbers and 1 tablespoon of the salt in a medium bowl. Cover with cold water; let stand 1 hour.

Drain cucumbers and return to bowl. In another medium bowl, combine sour cream, vinegar, sugar, onion, pepper and remaining 1/2 tablespoon salt; blend well. Stir sour cream mixture into cucumbers.

Cover bowl and refrigerate several hours before serving.

The thing I remember most about my mother's cooking is the one thing she could not do well —EGGS. But no one, including Hazel or Al Johnson, could make an egg in any manner that could be considered edible. My mother recognized this proclivity of mine early on and whenever she made potato salad, she always made two bowls; a small one for me and a big one (that included eggs) for everyone else.

One Easter I promised to eat a hard-boiled egg. Everyone else had finished their eggs as I was getting started (I had trouble with the shell) and left me sitting at the kitchen table. About 15 minutes later, my mother came back to the kitchen and got a big smile on her face when she saw there was no egg left on my plate. An hour or so later, she figured out why my plate had been wiped so clean. I think it had something to do with the smell that started to come from the back of the refrigerator where I had thrown the egg.

— E. John Larson
(author's brother)

Tartar Sauce

This tartar sauce is great with fish; however, we used it as a sandwich spread as well. My mom always made it for my brother John when he came home from college.

Yield: 2 cups

1 jar (16 ounces) mayonnaise
1 tablespoon grated onion
1/4 medium green pepper, chopped
1 tablespoon grated carrot
1 tablespoon grated celery
1/2 hard-boiled egg
1 tablespoon finely chopped pimento
2 tablespoons catsup
2 tablespoons chili sauce
1 tablespoon chopped parsley

Combine mayonnaise, onion, pepper, carrot, celery, egg, pimento, catsup, chili sauce and parsley in blender. Blend at low speed 45-60 seconds. Store tightly covered in refrigerator. Will keep several weeks.

Egg Gravy

This gravy was served whenever fried fish was the main course. It is also excellent over boiled potatoes.

Yield: 2 cups

4 tablespoons butter
4 tablespoons flour
1 teaspoon salt
1 teaspoon black pepper
2 cups milk
2 hard-boiled eggs, cut up

Melt butter in a small saucepan over low heat. Add flour, salt and pepper; stir until well blended. Gradually add milk, stirring constantly. Bring to a boil; continue to boil 2 minutes more, stirring occasionally. Stir in eggs until well coated. Serve immediately.

Baked White Beans

What would a picnic be without the baked beans?
These are simply the best you will ever eat.

Yield: 6-8 servings

1 pound navy beans
1 tablespoon salt
1 pound pork steak, cubed
1/4 cup brown sugar, packed
1 teaspoon dry mustard
1 tablespoon vinegar
1 small whole onion

Wash and soak beans in water in a large bowl several hours or overnight. Add extra water to ensure beans remain completely covered.

Drain and place beans in a large kettle. Cover with water and cook over low heat until skins burst, about 1 hour. Pour beans with liquid into bean pot. Add salt, pork, sugar, mustard and vinegar; mix well. Push onion in center of beans.

Cover and bake at 300 degrees for 4-5 hours. Add more water if beans begin to appear dry.

Hazel's first impression on me was a lasting one. It was in 1976 at Bernice's house where every relative from miles around was gathered to meet Jeanne's new boyfriend for the first time. When supper was served, Hazel passed the baked beans to me saying "beans, beans, the musical fruit— the more you eat the more you toot." It was her way of making me feel at ease, and it worked! Looking back, I never felt any other way in her company.

—Michael Hyde
(author's husband)

Fruit Cocktail Salad

It's old-fashioned, easy to prepare and graced the kitchen table many, many times.

Yield: 8 servings

  1 pint whipping cream
  1 tablespoon sugar
  1 can (32 ounces) fruit cocktail, drained
8-10 maraschino cherries, halved

Beat whipping cream in a deep bowl with electric mixer on high speed until slightly thick. Gradually add sugar; continue to beat until soft peaks are formed.

Fold fruit and cherries into whipped cream. Chill until ready to serve.

Cucumber Jello Salad

Molded salads were a mainstay of dinner in our homes back in the '50s and '60s. They were decorative and easy to transport to another family gathering.

Yield: 6 servings

  1 package (3 ounces) lime gelatin
3/4 cup hot water
  1 cup mayonnaise
  1 cup cottage cheese
  1 cup chopped nuts
  1 tablespoon chopped onion
  1 teaspoon lemon juice
  1 small cucumber, peeled, seeded and diced

Dissolve gelatin in water in a medium bowl. Refrigerate until nearly set; remove from refrigerator. Add mayonnaise, cottage cheese, nuts, onion, lemon juice and cucumber; blend well. Pour into jello mold. Chill until firm.

Rotamos

*The mild flavor of rutabagas
mashed together with potatoes is a perfect blend.
Vegetables were not a favorite of mine growing up,
but I never passed up this dish.*

Yield: 6 servings

 3 large potatoes
 1 large rutabaga
 1 tablespoon butter
 1 teaspoon salt
 1 teaspoon black pepper
 1/2 cup warm milk (approximate)

Peel and cut potatoes and rutabagas. Boil together in a large saucepan until fork-tender. Drain; return to pan and beat with electric mixer on medium speed until blended. Add butter, salt and pepper. Beat in milk until light and fluffy.

*Grandfather
John Larson (right).*

My grandpa's fishing boat in Appleport (probably some Larsons on there too). On Sundays I was told everyone dressed up (in white linen!), packed picnic baskets and went for a boat ride.

—Bev Knutson
(friend of author)

Baked Broccoli and Cheese

*If fresh broccoli is not available,
frozen broccoli can easily be substituted.
This dish has a soufflé-like texture.*

Yield: 6 servings

2 1/2 cups fresh broccoli, cut in small flowerets
1/4 cup chopped onion
2 tablespoons butter
2 tablespoons flour
1/2 cup water
8 ounces Colby cheese, cubed
3 eggs, beaten
1/2 cup crushed cornflakes

Preheat oven to 325 degrees. Place broccoli in a 2-quart ungreased casserole dish.

Sauté onion in butter in a medium saucepan until tender. Add flour and water; stir until thickened. Stir cheese into mixture until melted; add eggs. Pour cheese-egg mixture over broccoli. Sprinkle with cornflakes. Bake covered 30 minutes or until top is lightly browned.

7UP Salad

*This unlikely combination of ingredients creates a salad
that will delight everyone at the table.*

Yield: 4 servings

1 1/2 cups applesauce
1 package (3 ounces) lime gelatin
1 orange rind, grated
1 cup 7UP

Heat applesauce over low heat in a small saucepan. Add gelatin and stir until dissolved. Blend in orange rind and 7UP. Pour into a 1-quart mold and refrigerate until firm.

Carrot Casserole

Velveeta cheese makes a smooth, creamy sauce for these carrots. The potato chips add just the right crispness.

Yield: 6 servings

5 cups sliced carrots
1/2 teaspoon salt
1 small onion, chopped
4 tablespoons butter
8 ounces Velveeta cheese, cubed
1 cup crushed potato chips

Preheat oven to 350 degrees.

In a medium saucepan, cook carrots and salt in a small amount of water until carrots are nearly tender, about 10 minutes. Drain; return carrots to pan and add onion; mix well.

Spray a 2-quart casserole with nonstick cooking spray. Layer half of the carrot mixture in prepared dish. Dot with 2 tablespoons of the butter and half of the cheese. Spread remaining carrot mixture on top. Dot with remaining 2 tablespoons butter and cheese. Sprinkle chips on top. Bake covered for 45 minutes or until top is bubbly.

During the '40s, '50s and '60s, all the Larson relatives and friends would gather for a summer picnic at a beach, usually Sand Bay or North Bay. Later on they gathered at the Donald Larson cottage in Appleport. The men would fish the day before to have a good supply of fish, and the women would all bring their favorite dish or recipe. The outing lasted from noon until quite late in the evening. Then this was topped off by Hazel, Bernice, Mabel Larson, Lorraine Duclon and their husbands all playing cards at Hazel's until the wee hours of the morning. These picnics went on all summer long when vacation time was available. I was about 8 years old when I attended the first picnic (1943-1944). The last one at the Appleport cottage was about 1963.

—John M. Larson
(cousin of author)

Wilted Lettuce Salad

Yield: 4 servings

Wondering what to do with all that lettuce in your garden? Served with this bacon dressing will keep you going back for more.

6 cups lettuce
2 green onions, sliced
4 slices bacon
1/4 cup cider vinegar
2 tablespoons water
1 tablespoon sugar

Wash lettuce and pat dry with paper towel. Tear lettuce in pieces and place in a salad bowl. Sprinkle onions over lettuce.

Cut bacon in small pieces and fry in a small skillet until crisp. Remove to paper towel to drain. Add vinegar, water and sugar into skillet drippings. Heat to boiling, stirring constantly. When mixture has thickened, pour over lettuce and toss well. Serve immediately.

A spring ritual with Hazel was to go out into the fields to search for wild asparagus. She had a keen eye and was even able to spot a patch of it from the car. It was a great day when we found some in a newly discovered place. I've tried to carry on with this tradition.

—Richard Larson
(author's brother)

Nor-Ski Ridge
Fish Boil
with Recipes

Nor-Ski Ridge Fish Boil with Recipes

It was during his tour of duty in Germany that Hazel's son, Wink Larson, experienced the thrill of downhill skiing. Always a man of great vision (and dreams), he was able to turn his newfound passion into something that would be enjoyed by the entire county.

In 1958 Wink purchased some land just south of Fish Creek and started bringing his dream of a Door County ski hill closer to reality. It was a year of hard work, resourcefulness and determination. My dad, Emery Larson, loved tinkering with machinery and spent many days helping Wink set up tow ropes and ensuring that the other equipment

The Lodge in 1965.

was operating smoothly. He even made a snowcat out of an old tractor and other miscellaneous parts to groom the hills. Finally, there was something to do in the wintertime in Door County! We could come out of hibernation.

You didn't need to be a skier to enjoy Nor-Ski Ridge. From the newly built chalet, large windows provided a panoramic view of the slopes. More often than not, it was standing room only. Stopping at the ski hill was a requirement for many Sunday afternoon rides. Hot chocolate was served from a tricky dispenser—"Please only push the button ONCE!" read the sign. The food menu included soup, chili and hamburgers—all homemade. Hamburgers were sold for 25 cents.

While Nor-Ski Ridge's popularity continued to grow in the winter, it sat empty in the summer. But what could be done with a ski hill in warm weather? The Viking Restaurant in Ellison Bay was serving fish boils that began attracting tourists in increasing numbers. Various hotels also had occasional smaller boils. Elaine Johnson and Gretna Johns, the Nor-Ski cooks and Wink's partners in crime back then, helped develop the idea for serving Nor-Ski fish boils. They had learned the fish boiling technique from their mentor, Robbie Kodanko. He was a well-known character in the county, and he surely knew his

fish! Since the Viking Restaurant served whitefish and the supply was limited, trout became our fish of choice for the boils. Trout from Canada was delivered weekly by truck. Gretna and Elaine met the truck at their store in Sister Bay, the Beach Road Market, and handpicked the best trout for the fish boils. Lake Superior trout proved to be a winner. The coldness of Lake Superior waters kept the fish firm and their bright color made a fine presentation.

My dad on the snowcat.

Old Fashioned Door County Trout Boil

EVERY WEDNESDAY AND FRIDAY From 5:00 to 8:00

RAIN OR SHINE — EAT INDOORS OR OUT

NOR-SKI RIDGE

FISH CREEK, WISCONSIN

Fish boils at Nor-Ski Ridge began in the early '60s. Employees were primarily family members, although several friends helped out through the years. Gretna and Elaine handled the boiling duties the first two years, but because they dabbled in so many other enterprises, they later just supplied the fish. However, in those early days, I believe it was their merriment and storytelling skills that began drawing people to Nor-Ski. Combined with the wit and wisdom of Wink, this trio could entertain for hours on end. There was a camaraderie among them that made you feel part of the family. The bigger the audience around the boiling kettle, the more inventive their stories became. Tourists took home a rare bit of Door County lore. Fish boils were served on Wednesdays and Fridays and were $2.75 a plate. The dinner included trout, potatoes, onions, melted butter, coleslaw, pumpernickel bread, pickles and, of course, cherry pie à la mode. Coffee and Kool-Aid were offered as beverages. If there was extra fish from the boil, another piece was offered at no charge, as well as potatoes, coleslaw and bread. "Sorry, only one piece of pie please!" It was a rare occasion when there were leftovers.

Although Gretna and Elaine supplied the fish, it was up to us to bag them so they were easily accessible for the boils. The day or sometimes the morning before each boil, it was up to Audrey (Wink's wife), Hazel, my mom and me to peel the onions and potatoes. Then they were counted and bagged so they, too, were easily available. Although it was tedious work and the aroma of onions permeated the air, we never grew tired of one another's company. It was a chance to sit outside in the summer sun and catch up on the latest gossip. Wink's son, Mitch, had the least envied job of all. It was his chore to procure the firewood for the boil from Freddy Kodanko's woodpile. If the truck wasn't as full of wood as his father liked, Mitch would surely be reprimanded. It was also necessary to pile the wood at the ski hill "just so." Mitch persevered and eventually could handle any task given to him.

Wink had the awesome task of shredding the cabbage at Al Johnson's Restaurant in Sister Bay. It was done there because Al had a large shredding machine. Wink was always running "a little late" and sending him to Al's, his best friend since childhood, probably wasn't the best idea. Most of the time they got to talking too much, and the rest of us would get quite anxious waiting for him to get things started. Since Wink had replaced Gretna and Elaine as the Master Boiler, we couldn't do much without him. Someone also had to pick up the cherry pies and pumpernickel bread at Rudy's Bakery in Sister Bay. They were always made fresh the morning of the fish boils. Whoever was chosen to transport them to the ski hill had a most difficult task. The intoxicating aroma of the still-warm pies and bread was enough to send one off on some secluded side road and indulge in pure ecstasy.

It was my job to cut the many dozens of pies. They were usually cut into six pieces, but if we noticed the lines were getting particularly long, we could manage eight pieces.

Believe me, people did notice if their piece was smaller! At the same time Hazel was quietly stirring up her famous (and secret) recipe for coleslaw dressing, silverware was folded into napkins, butter was melting and the coffee began perking. Soon the fire pit outside was blazing, and the water in the black iron kettle began to boil.

Now we could assume our positions for the actual fish boil. Audrey positioned herself behind the desk near the entrance. She sold dinner tickets while skillfully persuading the reluctant to try it. (The thought of fish, onions and potatoes boiled together was considered disgusting by many people.) But once we went through the often tiresome litany of talking them into trying "just one piece," they were hooked. The next week we would see those same people bring their friends to "just try it." Audrey would then direct them outside to watch Wink and his able assistants create the fish boil "magic."

The highlight of any fish boil is the "boil over." Just before the fish are ready to be taken out, a small amount of kerosene is poured on the fire. This increases the heat, creates a huge flame and causes the water to boil over the kettle. This removes any salt or other impurities that may have settled on top. It's a spectacular sight with oohs and aahs similar to a Fourth of July fireworks display.

When the boil over reaches its finale, hungry patrons rush inside to be first in line. They are as eager for their fish as they are to see that wonderfully wrinkled lady standing on a box behind the counter who greets them and places the fish, potatoes and onions on their plates. That lady, of course, was Hazel. She made people feel as welcome at Nor-Ski as she would at her own home. Next to her, ladling out the melted butter and dishing up the coleslaw, was my mom. The laughter abounded and helped in making everyone feel at home. Unfamiliar faces became familiar faces, and many became very special friends; friendships that are lasting to this day.

In later years, we also offered pizza for the unadventurous ones (mainly children) who refused to try the fish. It was very hectic trying to coordinate a boil over and a baked pizza, especially now that we were serving up to 600 people a night. We didn't make everyone happy, but we did the best we could. It didn't help that Wink didn't always stick to his boiling schedule. He would be busy engaging in conversations and the oft-heard, panicked cry would go out—"WHERE'S WINK?!?"

Unfortunately, all good things come to an end. Wink sold Nor-Ski Ridge in 1970, and the fish boils ended in 1971. The unpredictability of Door County winters took its toll on the success of the ski hill. The fish boils, however, remained prosperous to the end. There were many reasons for its success—the excellent food, the beautiful setting and tourism was growing. But we will always believe the real reason that it flourished was the people that worked there. You felt welcome and appreciated. You laughed, and you also felt special—as though you were sitting with family at one big kitchen table.

The recipes included here are for eight servings. Everyone raved about Aunt Hazel's coleslaw—another recipe in which she would conveniently leave out an ingredient. I have tried to recreate that recipe to the best of my ability, but the real secret to her coleslaw was not in the ingredients. She always kept the dressing in a gallon jar in the refrigerator and wouldn't mix it up until just before each boil. This allowed the coleslaw to always stay fresh.

Fish Boil

Yield: 8 servings

 4 pounds small red potatoes
16 small white onions
10 quarts water
 1 cup salt, divided
 8 pounds trout, cut into 2-inch chunks

"Dishing it up."

Wash potatoes and cut a small slice off each end. Place in a bowl of cold water until ready to use. Peel onions.

Heat water in a large, deep kettle with strainer until boiling. Add potatoes, onions and 1/2 cup of the salt. When water returns to a rolling boil, boil 12 minutes. Add fish and remaining 1/2 cup salt. Return to rolling boil again; boil 11 minutes. (Do not overcook or fish will fall apart.) Lift strainer from water and drain. Rinse fish lightly and serve.

Coleslaw

Yield: 8 servings

8 cups shredded cabbage
2/3 cup salad dressing
2 teaspoons sugar
1 teaspoon lemon juice
1 teaspoon celery salt

Master Boiler Wink.

Place cabbage in a large bowl. Stir together salad dressing, sugar, lemon juice and celery salt in a small bowl. Pour over cabbage; blend well.

Cherry Pie

Yield: one 9-inch pie

Filling:
  2 tablespoons sugar
  5 teaspoons cornstarch
  1 cup cherry juice, divided
  1 tablespoon butter
  3 cups cherries, pitted

Crust:
  2 cups flour
  1/2 teaspoon salt
  2/3 cup shortening
  1/3 cup ice cold water
  1 tablespoon milk
  1 teaspoon sugar

To make filling, mix sugar, cornstarch and 1 teaspoon of the cherry juice in a small bowl; set aside.

In a medium saucepan, heat remaining scant 1 cup cherry juice to boiling. Add sugar mixture, stirring constantly until mixture is thickened. Remove from heat and stir in butter. Fold in cherries. Allow to cool while making pie crust.

Preheat oven to 425 degrees.

To prepare crust, sift flour and salt in a medium bowl. Cut shortening into flour with pastry blender until it resembles small peas. Add 1 tablespoon of water at a time, mixing lightly with a fork until all flour is moistened. Form into 2 equal balls.

Roll 1 ball into a 12-inch circle on a floured board. Fold dough in half and place in a 9-inch pie pan. Unfold dough and fit into pan. Trim to 1 inch beyond pie pan. Pour in cherry filling. Roll remaining dough in the same manner and place on top of cherries. Crimp edges together to seal. Cut 3 or 4 slits in top of crust. Brush top with milk and sprinkle with sugar. Bake 10 minutes. Reduce heat to 350 degrees and continue baking 45 minutes more or until crust is lightly browned and filling is bubbly.

My mom and Hazel always hosted a picnic for the cherry pickers (cherries were picked by hand then) at the end of the season. Homemade cherry pies were provided as dessert, and they enjoyed the "fruits of their labor."

Main Dishes

Oven-Baked Corned Beef

This traditional Irish recipe is perfect anytime of the year. It's so easy even a Swede can make it successfully.

Yield: 4 servings

5-6 pounds corned beef
2 cloves garlic, sliced
1 medium onion, sliced
1 green pepper, sliced
1 stalk celery, sliced
6 peppercorns
2 cloves
1 bay leaf
1 teaspoon dried rosemary
1 teaspoon dried parsley flakes
1 cup water

Preheat oven to 325 degrees. Line a roasting pan with heavy-duty aluminum foil.

Rinse corned beef, pat dry and place in prepared pan. Make six 1-inch cuts on top side of meat; put a slice of garlic in each cut. Spread onion, green pepper and celery over beef. Add peppercorns, cloves, bay leaf, rosemary, parsley flakes and water. Seal foil tightly.

Bake 4 hours or until meat is tender. Remove from oven; cool 10 minutes before slicing.

My mom and Hazel had completely different styles of cooking. My mom was the more traditional. She loved to scour newspapers and cookbooks for new ideas. Although she liked experimenting with different foods, she usually followed a recipe pretty closely. Hazel, on the other hand, liked to improvise. If she thought there might be a shortcut, she tried it—sometimes successfully, sometimes not. It always amazed me how she could serve up such a wonderful meal simply by using whatever might be in her pantry that day. I suppose that is one of the skills you acquired in the '30s and '40s when everything wasn't as plentiful as it is today.

Spanish Hamburgers

*Spanish Hamburgers were generally made for a
Saturday supper. The addition of my mom's homemade
buns and french fries made this meal special.
We couldn't get to the table fast enough
when she announced "Dinner's ready."*

Yield: 7-8 sandwiches

2 pounds ground beef
2 tablespoons vinegar
1 tablespoon lemon juice
1 tablespoon brown sugar
2 tablespoons Worcestershire sauce
1 cup diced celery
1 large onion, chopped
1 cup ketchup
1 cup water
1 teaspoon salt

Brown beef in a large skillet. Drain and return
beef to skillet. Add vinegar, lemon juice, sugar,
Worcestershire, celery, onion, ketchup, water
and salt. Bring to a boil; cover and simmer
1 hour.

Hazel sawin' the squash.

Swedish Spaghetti

*This was Aunt Hazel's most requested
spaghetti recipe—Swedish style.*

Yield: 4-5 servings

8 slices bacon, cubed
1/2 cup chopped onion
1/2 cup chopped celery
1/4 cup chopped green pepper
1 can (16 ounces) tomatoes
1 can (6 ounces) tomato paste
1 cup tomato juice
1 teaspoon salt
1 teaspoon black pepper
2 teaspoons sugar
1 box (7 ounces) macaroni spaghetti,
   cooked

Preheat oven to 350 degrees.

Fry bacon in a large skillet until crisp. Drain, reserving 2 tablespoons drippings. Return drippings to skillet and sauté onions, celery and green pepper until tender. Add tomatoes, tomato paste, tomato juice, bacon, salt, pepper and sugar to sauté mixture; mix well. Stir in spaghetti.

Pour into a 3-quart baking dish that has been sprayed with nonstick cooking spray. Bake covered 30 minutes.

Brown Rice Casserole

*Jarlsberg cheese gives this dish its unique flavor.
It's worth the trip to a gourmet shop to find it.
Try it as an accompaniment to grilled pork chops.
I guarantee this casserole won't make it
around the table twice.*

Yield: 4 servings

2 tablespoons butter
2 cups chopped onion
3 stalks celery, chopped
1/2 pound mushrooms, sliced
1/2 cup chopped fresh parsley
3 cups brown rice, cooked
2 cups shredded Jarlsberg cheese
1 teaspoon paprika
1 teaspoon black pepper
1/2 teaspoon ground ginger

Preheat oven to 350 degrees.

Melt butter in a medium skillet. Add onions, celery, mushrooms and parsley. Sauté until tender, about 10 minutes.

In a 3-quart baking dish that has been prepared with nonstick cooking spray, alternate layers of rice, saute mixture and cheese. Top with paprika, pepper and ginger.

Bake covered for 45 minutes.

My mom was always on the lookout for new recipes. While working at Koepsel's in Sister Bay, she met Adele Wolfe. Adele loved dabbling in gourmet cooking, and the two hit it off instantly. She also loved to laugh just as much as my mom. Their mutual love of cooking yielded a great and lasting friendship and many new recipes.

Spanish Rice

*This can be made as a side dish,
or add a loaf of warm bread
and it's a meal in itself.*

Yield: 4 servings

4-6 strips bacon, cubed
1 cup chopped onion
1/2 cup chopped green pepper
2 cloves garlic, chopped
1 can (14 ounces) whole tomatoes
1/2 teaspoon salt
1/2 teaspoon black pepper
1 cup rice, cooked
1/2 cup grated Cheddar cheese

Preheat oven to 350 degrees. Spray a medium baking dish with nonfat cooking spray.

Fry bacon in a large skillet until crisp. Drain; reserve 2 tablespoons drippings. Crumble bacon. Return drippings to skillet and add onion, green pepper and garlic; sauté 5 minutes. Stir in tomatoes, salt and pepper. Add rice and bacon; mix well.

Pour into a 3-quart baking dish; sprinkle with cheese. Bake covered 35-45 minutes or until bubbly.

Wild Rice Casserole

*Wild rice is plentiful in the early autumn
and can be found at many roadside stands.
This is one of the many wonderful recipes
that came from Betty Brown in Duluth.*

Yield: 8 servings

  3 cups water
1 1/2 cups wild rice
  2 beef bouillon cubes
  1 large onion, chopped
  2 cups celery, sliced
  2 tablespoons butter
  2 pounds hamburger, browned
  1 can (10 3/4 ounces) cream of mushroom
     soup
  1 can (10 3/4 ounces) cream of chicken soup
  1 cup chicken broth
  1 cup water chestnuts, sliced
  2 tablespoons soy sauce
  1 package (16 ounces) noodles, cooked

Bring water to a boil in a medium saucepan.
Add rice and bouillon cubes; simmer 45 minutes. Drain and rinse rice.

Sauté onion and celery in butter in a large skillet. Add hamburger and mix well. Stir in soups,
broth, water chestnuts and rice. Add soy sauce;
cook until heated through. Serve over noodles.

The twins, Emery and Everett.

Grandma's Last Wish

*E*mery and Everett were commercial fishermen, and they operated off the old family dock. This was quite a dock, with a length of over 500 feet. In the spring of 1992, while having coffee and cookies at Grandma's she said, "Let's rebuild the old dock!" I looked a little puzzled at her, but I knew she meant it. In July construction began. I lined up someone to build the cribs and bought 250 truckloads of fill from a large construction job; and by Christmas that year we had a 500-foot dock. Why would an 83-year-old woman want to see a dock rebuilt? I think it was her way of bringing back some of the past. I think of my grandma every day.

—Mitch Larson
(Hazel's grandson)

Fresh Door County Baked Whitefish

Whitefish is a Door County specialty! My mom and Aunt Hazel made sure they were in Sand Bay when Lee Peterson came in with his fishing boat. You can't get fish fresher than that! This dish will bring back those special memories of Door County.

Yield: 8 servings

1 whitefish (4-5 pounds)
2 teaspoons salt
1 medium onion, sliced
1 teaspoon paprika
1 cup milk (approximate)

Preheat oven to 375 degrees. Spray a 13x9-inch baking dish with nonstick cooking spray.

Rinse fish under cold running water; pat dry. Place fish in prepared pan and rub inside with salt. Lay onions on top of fish and sprinkle with paprika. Add milk to approximately 1/2-inch depth in pan. Bake 45 minutes.

Note: Leaving the head on the whitefish is optional.

Pan-Fried Perch

There was always a debate whether perch was more flavorful fried with the bones or filleted. My mom and Aunt Hazel insisted "with the bones" was best. I sometimes wonder if that was because they had to clean the fish.

Yield: 5-6 servings

2 pounds fresh perch
1 cup flour
1 teaspoon salt
1 teaspoon black pepper
1/4 cup shortening

Rinse fish under cold running water and place on paper towel; pat dry. Combine flour, salt, and pepper in a pie tin. Dredge perch in flour mixture, turning over to coat both sides; set on waxed paper.

Melt shortening to cover approximately 1/8 inch of bottom of a large skillet. Lay perch in a single layer and fry 3-4 minutes or until golden brown. Carefully turn and fry until golden brown or until fish flakes easily with fork; drain on paper towel. (It is important to turn fish over only once while frying.)

I think some of the great fried fish I had at Hazel's was due to that cast iron skillet of hers.

—Dorothy Bonow
(a regular at Hazel's
kitchen table)

Hazel cleaning fish.

Holiday Baked Ham

Any holiday was reason enough for ham.
Even though Hazel's table was used for many
occasions, Christmas and Easter meals
were usually served at our home.
This ham is mouthwatering.

Yield: 8-10 servings

1	bone-in ham (5-6 pounds)
10-12	whole cloves
1	can (6 ounces) sliced pineapple
2-3	cups 50/50 soda
1/2	cup brown sugar
1	teaspoon dry mustard

Preheat oven to 325 degrees.

Make crisscross slices, about 1/4 inch deep, on top and sides of ham; insert cloves into slices. Place ham in large baking pan. Drain pineapple; reserve juice and lay slices on top of ham. Pour 1 cup 50/50 over ham. Bake in oven, allowing 20-25 minutes per pound. Baste with remaining 50/50 about every 30 minutes.

Meanwhile, combine brown sugar and mustard in a small bowl. Stir in enough pineapple juice to make mixture pourable. Pour over entire ham the last 30 minutes of baking. Bake until ham is heated through or according to baking times on label.

Kroppkaker

*Kroppkaker is the Swedish name for what we always referred to as "**Cannonballs**"; that is exactly what they look like. We jokingly said that's what they felt like after you ate them. It was difficult to find a spot at the table when Hazel was making Cannonballs.*

Yield: 6 servings

2	pounds pork shoulder, finely chopped
4	teaspoons finely chopped onion
1 1/2	teaspoons salt, divided
6	large potatoes
4	tablespoons dry instant mashed potatoes
1/3	cup flour
1/4	teaspoon baking powder

Fry pork, onion, and 1/2 teaspoon of the salt in a medium skillet until golden brown; set aside.

Using a meat grinder, grind potatoes into a large bowl. Transfer potatoes to strainer. Remove all moisture by pressing potatoes against sides of strainer (using your hands or the back of a spoon). Continue pressing until potatoes are dry, about 30-35 times. Return potatoes to bowl and add instant mashed potatoes, flour and baking powder. Stir until dough is formed. Shape dough into 6 patties; place 1 teaspoon meat filling in center. Wrap dough around filling to form a ball.

Fill a large kettle 3/4 full of water. Add remaining salt and bring to a boil. Add Cannonballs and gently boil 45 minutes. (Cannonballs will sink to bottom of kettle during the first 20 minutes of cooking.) Remove cooked balls with slotted spoon and place on platter. Serve with melted butter or a rich cream sauce.

Over the years, I had many cooking lessons in my Grandma Hazel's kitchen. To prove it, I have five different versions of the Cannonball recipe. Interestingly, each version is slightly different from the one before. Although I took detailed notes, to this day I do not believe I will be able to make the recipe quite like my grandma could. There are simply no words to describe how coarse to grind the potatoes or how much water to strain from the ground potatoes. Whether I ever intended to learn to make Cannonballs, I am not sure. I do know the true enjoyment was in the lessons.

*—Lisa Larson Mandelin
(Hazel's granddaughter)*

Potato Sausage

*It is difficult to find anyone
who still makes potato sausage today.
When I was growing up in Appleport,
it was a frequent meal for us.
It is delicious as a main course
or sliced cold the next day.*

Yield: 6 servings

1 pound pork casings
5 pounds potatoes, peeled
1 large onion, quartered
5 pounds ground pork
5 pounds ground beef
6 tablespoons salt
1 teaspoon black pepper
1 teaspoon allspice
1 cup water

Prepare casings for stuffing by soaking in cold water about 1 hour. This removes the salt in the casings.

Boil potatoes and onion in a large stock pot for 5 minutes. Remove from heat and cool. Grind potatoes and onion together in a meat grinder (use plate with smallest holes).

Combine potato mixture, pork, beef, salt, pepper and allspice in a large bowl; blend well. Mix in water as needed to make mixture very moist.

Rinse casings and cut into three 18-inch lengths. Stuff potato mixture into casings using a meat grinder with the sausage stuffer attachment or a wide-mouthed funnel. Do not over-stuff, as mixture expands during cooking. Tie each end with string. Ends may be tied together to form rings. At this point, sausage may be cooked or frozen.

(continued)

To cook sausage, place in a large pan half filled with water. Carefully prick small holes in sausages with a needle to prevent bursting. Bring sausages to a boil; reduce heat to simmer and cook uncovered for 1 hour.

Note: Pork casings are available at most butcher shops.

Lisa, Roger and me.

Crescent Sausage Cheese Bake

This was a dish my mom prepared quite often when I came home with my family for the weekend. It was a meal she could prepare ahead of time and just pop into the oven when we arrived.

Yield: 4 servings

1 package (8 ounces) crescent dinner rolls
1 package (8 ounces) brown and serve
    sausages, sliced
2 cups shredded Monterey Jack cheese
4 eggs, slightly beaten
3/4 cup milk
2 tablespoons chopped green pepper
1/2 teaspoon salt
1/4 teaspoon black pepper
1/4 teaspoon oregano

Preheat oven to 425 degrees.

Press dough into an ungreased 13x9-inch pan. Place sausages over dough; sprinkle with cheese.

Combine eggs, milk, green pepper, salt, pepper and oregano in a medium bowl; mix until well blended. Pour over cheese. Bake covered 20-25 minutes.

For a couple of years Aunt Hazel's grandchildren, Lisa and Mitch, and I would get her house ready for her return home in the spring. One time we turned everything backwards and scattered footprints across her ceiling. But her favorite "welcome home" was when we filled her entire bathroom with crumpled newspapers. There was also a "stuffed gentleman" waiting for her in the living room. Aunt Hazel promptly named him Roger, and he kept her company the entire summer. Roger was even seen riding on a float in the Fall Festival parade!

Swedish Oven Pancake

One of the favorite meals my mom and
Aunt Hazel shared was an oven pancake.
They were always making dinner for each other
and sharing the hottest topics of the day.

Yield: 6 servings

1/2 cup butter
3 eggs
3 cups milk
2 cups flour
1 teaspoon salt

Preheat oven to 350 degrees.

Melt butter in a 12-inch ovenproof skillet. Whisk eggs in a medium bowl until well beaten. Add milk; whisk until blended. Combine flour and salt; add to egg mixture.

Pour batter into prepared skillet and bake 1 hour. (Pancake will rise in the beginning, but will fall as it continues to bake.) Remove skillet from oven; cut pancake in pie-shaped wedges or slices and serve with butter and syrup.

Sister Bay Moravian Church
Sunday School, 1956.
(Third from left—
Jeanne Hyde–author)

Lutefisk

Lutefisk is a legendary Scandinavian dish of cod fish that has been treated with lye. It also has a legendary taste and smell. This recipe is not for the faint of heart. There are two ways to prepare lutefisk— boiled or baked. Baked will give your kitchen a little better aroma.

Yield: 4-6 servings

Boiled:
 2-3 pounds lutefisk
   1 cheesecloth

Rinse and soak fish several hours or overnight in a large bowl of water.

Bring a large kettle of water to a boil; wrap fish in cheesecloth and place in kettle. Return water to a boil and boil 5-10 minutes or until fish flakes easily with a fork. Remove fish from water and drain. Serve with melted butter or cream sauce.

Baked:
 2-3 pounds lutefisk
   2 cups water
   1 teaspoon salt

Preheat oven to 400 degrees.

Rinse lutefisk in cold water and soak several hours or overnight in a large bowl.

Drain well; place in a 13x9-inch baking dish (not aluminum). Add water and salt; cover with foil. Bake 20 minutes or until fish flakes easily with a fork. Serve with melted butter or Cream Sauce.

When Jeanne and I were kids, the only way we knew it was Easter season was when we came home from school and we could smell the scent of home perms our mothers gave each other. The good news was the smell of lutefisk was gone, but we felt terror because we knew that we were next for home perms—roll 'em tight so it lasts!

—Bev Knutson
(friend of author)

(continued)

Cream Sauce

Yield: 1 cup

2 tablespoons butter
2 tablespoons flour
1 cup hot milk
1/4 teaspoon salt
1/4 teaspoon black pepper

Melt butter over low heat in a small saucepan. Blend in flour; gradually stir in milk. Add salt and pepper; stir until sauce is boiling and smooth. Serve hot over cooked lutefisk.

Swedish Hash (Putt i Panna)

This is a great way to use leftover beef roast. It's an old Swedish recipe that's good for breakfast, lunch or dinner.

Yield: 4 servings

2 medium onions, chopped
4 tablespoons butter
2 cups diced leftover beef roast
7-8 cold cooked medium potatoes, diced
1 teaspoon salt
1 teaspoon black pepper

Cook onions in butter in a large skillet until tender. Add roast beef, potatoes, salt and pepper. Cook over medium heat, turning occasionally with a spatula until browned, but not dry.

Back in the 1950s, Sister Bay had its own fresh fish market called Salty Joe's. Joe D'Loughy ran an excellent business, but he had his own way of handling customers. One day a woman entered the store requesting a fresh fish. Salty Joe showed her one from the showcase. "Do you have a bigger fish?" she asked. "Sure," Salty Joe replied. "I have another in the back." So he carried the one he was holding into the back, filled its mouth with ice chunks, brought it back out and set the fish on the scale. It weighed about 3/4 of a pound more. "That's just the size I wanted!" exclaimed the woman and left the store as one more satisfied customer.

—contributed by Gretna and Elaine (friends at Hazel's kitchen table)

Cakes and Cookies

It makes a birthday special.

My Aunt Bernice was the finest cake baker I ever met. She had baking down to an art. It was tradition to receive her Sour Cream Chocolate cake for every birthday. I doubt anyone ever turned down that offer. Fortunately, her daughter Jeanne did learn to make it and maybe, if we ask, she will continue the tradition for birthdays.

—Lisa Larson Mandelin
(Hazel's granddaughter)

Lessons From My Mom

"You must cream the butter and sugar with your hands," my mom said. That was her secret in making such a rich, moist cake. "The warmth of your hands makes a much lighter, creamier mixture." I still follow her advice to this day.

Sour Cream Chocolate Cake

This is by far the most requested birthday cake in Door County. If you didn't get a piece when the candles were blown out, you had to wait until the next birthday. It must be frosted with White Birthday Cake Frosting (page 71).

Yield: one 9-inch layer cake

2 squares (1 ounce each) unsweetened
    baking chocolate
1/2 cup water
1/2 cup (1 stick) butter
1 1/2 cups sugar
2 cups cake flour
1 teaspoon baking soda
1/4 teaspoon salt
3 eggs
1 cup sour cream
1 teaspoon vanilla extract

Preheat oven to 350 degrees. Spray two round 9-inch pans with nonstick cooking spray.

In a small pan, melt chocolate in water. Stir until thick; set aside to cool.

In a large bowl, cream butter and sugar with electric mixer on medium-high speed until light and creamy. Sift flour, baking soda and salt together twice. Add to creamed mixture along with eggs and sour cream. Beat with electric mixer on medium-high speed for 2 minutes. Add chocolate and vanilla; beat 2 minutes more.

Divide batter evenly into prepared pans. Bake 30-35 minutes. Remove from oven and cool in pans 2 minutes. Remove from pans onto wire racks and continue cooling. Slice each layer in half and frost layers, sides and top with White Birthday Cake Frosting.

Maraschino Cherry Cake

This was a favorite to bring to picnics or the PTA meetings at Appleport School.

Yield: one 13x9-inch cake
12-15 servings

1 cup sugar
1/2 cup shortening
1 egg
1 square (1 ounce) unsweetened baking
   chocolate, melted
2 cups flour
1 teaspoon baking soda
1 cup sour milk
1/2 cup maraschino cherries, finely chopped
1/2 cup maraschino cherry juice
1/2 cup nuts

Preheat oven to 350 degrees. Spray a 13x9-inch cake pan with nonstick cooking spray.

In a large bowl, cream sugar and shortening with electric mixer on medium-high speed until fluffy. Add egg and chocolate. Sift flour and baking soda together. Add flour mixture (about 1/3 at a time) alternately with sour milk to batter. Beat well after each addition. Stir in cherries, cherry juice and nuts.

Pour into prepared pan. Bake 35 minutes or until wooden pick inserted in center comes out clean.

Note: This is excellent with Quick Fudge Frosting (page 72).

Orange Cake

A simple cake, but oh so flavorful!
The raisins keep the cake moist, and the
brown sugar glaze just melts in your mouth.

Yield: 12 servings

Cake:
- 1/2 cup water, very hot
- 1 cup raisins
- 2 cups flour
- 1 teaspoon baking soda
- 1 cup sugar
- 1/2 cup shortening
- 1 egg
- 1 orange rind, grated
- 1 cup sour milk*

Glaze:
- 3/4 cup brown sugar
- 2 tablespoons orange juice

Preheat oven to 350 degrees. Spray a 13x9-inch cake pan with nonstick cooking spray.

Combine water and raisins in a small bowl. Allow to soak while preparing cake. In a medium bowl, sift flour and baking soda together; set aside.

Cream sugar and shortening in a large bowl until light and fluffy, about 3-5 minutes. Add egg and orange rind; mix well. Add flour mixture (about 1/3 at a time) alternately with milk to mixture. Mix well after each addition. Drain raisins and add to mixture. Pour into prepared pan. Bake 30-35 minutes or until cake springs back when lightly touched in center.

Prepare glaze by combining brown sugar and orange juice in a small bowl; mix well. Spread glaze over cake while still hot.

*Note: Make sour milk by adding 1 tablespoon lemon juice or distilled white vinegar to a scant 1 cup of milk.

Rum Cake

Aunt Hazel always had a lot of fun baking this cake.
Gee, I wonder why?

Yield: 6-8 servings

Cake:
- 1 cup walnuts, chopped
- 1 package (18$^{1}/_{2}$ ounces) yellow cake mix
- 1 package (3$^{3}/_{4}$ ounces) instant vanilla pudding
- 4 eggs
- $^{1}/_{2}$ cup cold water
- $^{1}/_{2}$ cup salad oil
- $^{1}/_{2}$ cup rum

Glaze:
- $^{1}/_{2}$ cup (1 stick) butter
- $^{1}/_{4}$ cup water
- 1 cup sugar
- $^{1}/_{2}$ cup rum

Preheat oven to 350 degrees. Spray a Bundt cake pan with nonstick cooking spray. Sprinkle nuts on bottom of pan.

In a large bowl, beat cake mix, dry pudding mix, eggs, water, oil and rum with electric mixer on medium speed until well blended, about 3-5 minutes. Pour batter over nuts in pan; bake 1 hour. Remove cake from oven and invert onto serving plate.

To prepare glaze, melt butter in a medium saucepan; stir in water and sugar. Bring to a boil; boil 5 minutes, stirring occasionally. Stir in rum. Drizzle glaze over top of cake.

Old-Fashioned Oatmeal Cake

A cake that will satisfy your sweet craving without being too sweet. My dad often included a piece (or pieces) in his late evening snack. Although he usually poured evaporated milk over his, I wouldn't recommend it.

Yield: one 13x9-inch cake
12 servings

Cake:
1 1/2 cups boiling water
1 1/4 cups oatmeal
1/2 cup shortening
1 cup granulated sugar
1 cup brown sugar
2 eggs
1 teaspoon cinnamon
1 1/2 cups flour
1/2 teaspoon salt
1 teaspoon baking soda

Icing:
6 tablespoons butter, softened
1/2 cup brown sugar
1 teaspoon vanilla extract
1 cup coconut
1/2 cup nuts, chopped
1/4 cup evaporated milk (approximately)

My dad, Emery Larson.

My dad usually ate his fourth meal of the day just before bedtime. Sometimes it consisted of a can of sardines and crackers, a sandwich or leftovers. This not being enough, a piece of cake with plenty of canned milk poured over it pleased him immensely. He would also be sure to let us know that he "never gained an ounce." He "weighed the same as the day he joined the Coast Guard in 1943."

In a medium bowl, pour boiling water over oatmeal. Let stand 20 minutes.

Preheat oven to 375 degrees. Spray a 13x9-inch cake pan with nonstick cooking spray.

Cream shortening and sugars in a large bowl until light, about 2-3 minutes. Add eggs and beat well; stir in oatmeal. Sift together cinnamon, flour, salt and baking soda; stir into batter. Spread batter into prepared pan. Bake 35-40 minutes or until wooden pick inserted in center comes out clean.

(continued)

Prepare icing by combining butter, brown sugar, vanilla, coconut and nuts in a small bowl. Stir in milk to desired consistency.

Preheat broiler; spread icing over top of baked cake and broil until icing is bubbly. (This only takes 1-2 minutes, so watch very carefully!) Remove cake from broiler and cool on wire rack.

Pear Cake

My Aunt Hazel made this cake using pears left on her back porch by anonymous donors. Anonymous, that is, until the cake was ready.

Yield: 6 servings

2 eggs
1 1/2 cups sugar
2 teaspoons vanilla extract
1/2 cup flour
2 teaspoons baking powder
1/4 teaspoon salt
1 cup nuts, chopped
1 cup pears, chopped

Preheat oven to 350 degrees. Spray an 8x8-inch cake pan with nonstick cooking spray.

In a medium bowl, beat eggs thoroughly with electric mixer on medium-high speed. Add sugar and vanilla.

Sift together flour, baking powder and salt in a small bowl. Blend into egg mixture. Add nuts and pears; mix well. Spread evenly into prepared pan. Bake 25 minutes or until golden brown. May be served warm or cold and topped with whipped cream.

Streusel Coffee Cake

Make this for a Sunday brunch or midweek coffee break.

Yield: 4-6 servings

Cake:
- 1 1/2 cups flour
- 3 teaspoons baking powder
- 1/4 teaspoon salt
- 3/4 cup sugar
- 1/4 cup shortening
- 1 egg, well beaten
- 1/2 cup milk

Streusel:
- 1/2 cup brown sugar
- 2 teaspoons cinnamon
- 2 teaspoons flour
- 2 tablespoons butter, softened
- 1/2 cup nuts, chopped

Powdered sugar frosting:
- 1 cup powdered sugar, sifted
- 1-2 teaspoons water
- 1/2 teaspoon vanilla extract

Preheat oven to 350 degrees. Spray an 8x8-inch cake pan with nonstick cooking spray.

In a medium bowl, sift together flour, baking powder, salt and sugar. Cut shortening into flour mixture with a pastry blender until it resembles small peas. Blend in egg and milk.

To make streusel, in a medium bowl, combine brown sugar, cinnamon, flour and butter. Stir in nuts.

Spread half the batter into prepared pan. Sprinkle with half the streusel mixture. Cover with remaining batter. Sprinkle remaining streusel on top. Bake 25 minutes or until wooden pick inserted in center comes out clean. Remove from oven and cool on wire rack.

(continued)

Prepare powdered sugar frosting by combining powdered sugar, water and vanilla in a small bowl. Stir until slightly runny (adding more water, if necessary) and drizzle over cake.

Chocolate Angel Food Cake

Imported cocoa gives this cake its rich chocolate flavor. Once my mom discovered this, it became a personal favorite of hers. How about some Wild Strawberry Frosting (page 70) on a piece of this?

Yield: 8-10 servings

3/4 cup cake flour
1 1/2 cups powdered sugar
1/3 cup Dutch processed cocoa
2 teaspoons instant espresso coffee
1 1/2 cups egg whites (10-12 eggs)
1/4 teaspoon salt
1/2 teaspoon cream of tartar
1 cup granulated sugar

Preheat oven to 375 degrees.

In a large bowl, sift together flour, powdered sugar, cocoa and coffee. Sift 2 more times; set aside.

Beat egg whites, salt and cream of tartar in another large bowl with electric mixer on medium-high speed until foamy, about 2 minutes. Gradually add granulated sugar and continue beating until stiff peaks are formed. (Do not overbeat.)

Carefully fold in flour mixture, making sure there are no air pockets. Gently spoon batter into an ungreased 10-inch tube pan. Bake 35-40 minutes or until golden brown. Remove cake from oven and immediately invert onto a long-necked bottle. Cool completely, about 1 1/2-2 hours and remove from pan.

Jelly Roll

*Jelly Rolls were quite popular in the '40s and '50s.
Aunt Hazel made many in her lifetime.
When you saw the bulging rolled towel
with a lot of powdered sugar over it,
you knew she had just baked another one.
The filling was usually whatever homemade
jelly or jam she had on hand.*

Yield: 10-12 servings

6 egg yolks
1 cup sugar
1 1/2 cups cake flour
1/2 teaspoon salt
2 teaspoons baking powder
6 tablespoons orange juice
1 cup jelly
2 tablespoons powdered sugar

Preheat oven to 350 degrees. Spray a cookie sheet with nonstick cooking spray and line with waxed paper.

In a large bowl, beat egg yolks with electric mixer on medium speed until thick and lemon colored, about 10 minutes. Gradually add sugar while continuing to beat yolks; stir in vanilla. Sift together flour, salt and baking powder. Add alternately to batter (about 1/2 at a time) with orange juice; beat 2 minutes.

Pour batter onto prepared cookie sheet and bake 20-25 minutes or until cake springs back when lightly touched in center.

Remove cake from oven and peel off waxed paper. Turn onto a clean damp cloth that has been lightly dusted with powdered sugar. Trim off edges. Spread top of cake with your favorite jelly. Carefully roll up cake, starting at the widest side.

Note: Any favorite jelly may be used as filling.

My greatest memories of Hazel are playing a non-ending game of cards called "spite and malice." She kept a blackboard on the kitchen wall where we kept a continuous record of who owed who, which we never paid. It still hangs there with "H" owing "A" $1.40.

—Audrey Larson Schram
(Hazel's daughter-in-law)

Daffodil Cake

*Light and sweet just as the name implies,
it's a perfect party or birthday cake.*

Yield: 8-10 servings

1$1/2$ cups sugar
$2/3$ cup water
6 eggs, separated
$1/2$ teaspoon salt
1 teaspoon cream of tartar
1$1/6$ cups cake flour, sifted and divided
$1/2$ teaspoon vanilla extract
$1/4$ teaspoon almond extract
$1/2$ teaspoon orange extract

Preheat oven to 325 degrees.

Combine sugar and water in a medium saucepan; bring to a boil. Cook without stirring until mixture reaches thread stage or 234 degrees on a candy thermometer.

Beat egg whites in a deep bowl with electric mixer on high speed until foamy, about 2 minutes. Add salt and cream of tartar; continue beating until stiff peaks are formed. Gradually pour sugar syrup over egg whites, beating constantly until mixture is cool.

Divide batter in half and place in 2 medium bowls. Fold $1/2$ cup of the flour into first bowl. Carefully stir in vanilla and almond extracts. Beat egg yolks in second bowl; fold in remaining $2/3$ cup flour and orange extract.

Alternately spoon batters into an ungreased 10-inch tube pan. Bake 1 hour or until cake springs back when lightly touched. Remove from oven and carefully invert pan onto a long-necked bottle. Cool completely, about 1$1/2$-2 hours.

Cherry Torte

*A summer in Door County wouldn't be complete
without fresh cherries. This is a great alternative to pie.
This recipe is from my aunt, Grace Landstrom.*

Yield: 6 servings

Cake:
- 1 cup sugar
- 1 tablespoon butter, softened
- 1 egg, beaten
- 1 tablespoon cherry juice
- 1 cup flour
- 1/2 teaspoon salt
- 1/2 teaspoon baking soda
- 1 teaspoon cinnamon
- 2 cups cherries, drained (reserve juice)
- 1/2 cup nuts, chopped

Sauce:
- 2 cups cherry juice
- 1/2 cup sugar
- 2 tablespoons cornstarch
- 1/8 teaspoon salt
- 1 tablespoon butter

Preheat oven to 350 degrees. Spray a 9x9-inch pan with nonstick cooking spray.

Combine sugar, butter, egg and cherry juice in a medium bowl. Beat with electric mixer on medium speed until creamy, about 2 minutes.

In a small bowl, sift together flour, salt, baking soda and cinnamon. Add to creamed mixture and blend well. Stir in cherries and nuts. Pour into prepared pan and bake 45 minutes or until wooden pick inserted in center comes out clean. Remove from oven and set on wire rack to cool.

To prepare sauce, combine cherry juice, sugar and cornstarch in a medium saucepan. Cook over medium heat until thick. Remove from heat and stir in salt and butter. Pour warm sauce over cake when served.

Al Johnson began spending summers in Appleport in the late 1930s. He met Hazel while picking cherries for the Larsons. He had to be in the orchard some days as early as 3:30 a.m. to earn the tremendous sum of 2 1/2 cents a pail! "There were a couple of Swedish fellows also picking cherries who lived in Appleport, and they would sing Swedish songs while filling their pails," Al recalls. "Hazel loved that because she understood Swedish."

Rice Pudding

We wouldn't be Swedish if we didn't make Rice Pudding. It's very creamy with just a hint of spices. My aunt, Grace Landstrom, usually "surprised" me with this on my birthday—she made the best.

Yield: 6-8 servings

 1 cup rice
 2 cups water
 3 cups milk
 4 eggs
1/4 cup sugar
1/4 cup butter, melted
1/2 teaspoon salt
 1 cup raisins (optional)
 1 tablespoon butter
1/2 teaspoon cinnamon
1/8 teaspoon nutmeg

Preheat oven to 325 degrees.

Boil rice and water in a large saucepan until all water has been absorbed, about 15 minutes. Add milk and simmer until milk has been absorbed.

In a medium bowl, beat eggs thoroughly with electric mixer on medium speed. Gradually beat together sugar, butter and salt. Stir into rice mixture; add raisins. Pour into a medium casserole dish. Top with dots of butter and sprinkle with cinnamon and nutmeg. Bake 1 hour or until browned on top. May be served hot or cold.

Danish Layer Cake

What a presentation this cake makes!
It may take a little extra effort,
but you will still be getting compliments
long after it's gone ... which won't be long.

Yield: 20-24 servings

Cake:
    12 eggs, separated
     2 cups sugar, divided
     1 teaspoon vanilla extract
     2 cups flour
     2 teaspoons baking powder
    1/2 teaspoon salt
     1 cup raspberry jam

Custard:
    3/4 cup sugar
    1/4 teaspoon salt
     8 teaspoons cornstarch
     3 egg yolks, beaten
     2 cups milk
     1 teaspoon vanilla extract
     2 tablespoons butter

Frosting:
     4 tablespoons flour
     1 cup milk
     1 cup (2 sticks) butter
     1 cup sugar
     1 teaspoon vanilla extract

Preheat oven to 350 degrees. Spray 4 Danish layer cake tins (or cookie sheets) with nonstick cooking spray and line with waxed paper.

Combine egg yolks, 1 1/2 cups of the sugar and vanilla in a large bowl. Beat with electric mixer at medium-high speed until thick and creamy, about 5-7 minutes. Sift together flour, baking powder and salt; add to egg yolk mixture and stir until blended.

(continued)

In another large bowl, beat egg whites at high speed until frothy, about 2 minutes. Gradually add remaining 1/2 cup sugar and continue beating until stiff peaks are formed, about 5 minutes. Carefully fold into egg yolk batter. Spread batter into prepared pans and bake 10 minutes or until golden brown. Remove from oven and cool on wire racks.

To prepare custard, combine sugar, salt and cornstarch in the top of a double boiler. In bottom pan of double boiler, add 1 inch of water and bring to a boil. Add egg and milk to sugar mixture. Cook over boiling water until thickened, stirring constantly, about 5 minutes. Stir in vanilla and butter. Remove from heat and allow to cool in pan.

To prepare frosting, dissolve flour in milk in a small saucepan. Cook over medium heat until thick, stirring constantly. Remove from heat and cool. Cream butter and sugar in a medium bowl; add flour mixture and vanilla. Beat until light and fluffy, about 10 minutes.

To assemble cake, place first layer on a large cake plate. Spread half of custard on top. Place second layer on custard and spread jam over layer. Top with third layer and spread with remaining custard. Set last layer on top and frost sides and top of cake. Additional jam may be swirled on top, if desired.

Blitz Torte

Blitz means "lightning" in German.
This torte will be devoured as quick as lightning.

Yield: 6-8 servings

1 cup flour
1 teaspoon baking powder
1 teaspoon salt
1/2 cup (1 stick) butter
11/2 cups sugar, divided
5 eggs, separated (reserve 1 yolk for filling)
1 teaspoon vanilla extract
7 teaspoons milk
1/2 cup sliced blanched almonds

Filling:
21/4 teaspoons cornstarch
3 teaspoons sugar
1/4 teaspoon salt
1 cup milk
1 egg yolk
1 teaspoon vanilla extract

Preheat oven to 350 degrees. Spray two 9-inch round cake pans with nonstick cooking spray.

In a small bowl, sift together flour, baking powder and salt; set aside. In a large bowl, cream butter and 1/2 cup of the sugar with electric mixer on medium-high speed. Beat 4 of the egg yolks in a separate bowl and add to creamed mixture along with vanilla, milk and flour mixture; mix until well blended. Divide batter evenly into prepared pans.

Beat egg whites until frothy in a medium bowl, about 2 minutes. Gradually add remaining 1 cup sugar and beat until stiff peaks are formed, about 5 minutes more. Divide evenly and spread over batter; sprinkle almonds on

(continued)

top. Bake 30 minutes or until golden brown. (Prepare filling while cake is baking.) Remove from oven and cool 10 minutes in pans; remove cake from pans and continue cooling on wire racks.

To make filling, thoroughly combine cornstarch, sugar and salt in top of double boiler. Bring 1 inch of water to boil in bottom of double boiler. Add milk and remaining egg yolk to cornstarch mixture; stir constantly. Cook over boiling water until thick; add vanilla. Cool in pan.

To assemble cake, set first layer on cake plate, meringue side up. Spread filling over layer. Top with second layer, meringue side up.

Hazel used to telephone and tell me her coffee was a week or so old waiting for me to share it. I knew she'd have a fresh pot of coffee made and would plug it in when she saw my car come in the driveway.

—Lucy Witalison
(a regular at
Hazel's kitchen table)

No berry, wild or tame, was safe from being picked and made into a jam or jelly. Our favorite, though, was wild strawberries. I had to trek out into the field with the rest of the family to spend the day looking for those tiny berries. Although the others seemed to quickly fill their pint jars, mine would never quite reach half full. The red stains around my mouth were a telltale sign. Wild strawberries make the sweetest jam, but the cup or so we needed to make Wild Strawberry Frosting was enjoyed the most.

Wild Strawberry Frosting

*This is my favorite frosting!
It's excellent on any type sponge cake.
Try it sandwiched between graham crackers—
you can't go wrong.*

Yield: 4 cups frosting

1 cup wild strawberries
1 cup sugar
1 egg white

Combine strawberries, sugar and egg white in a large bowl. Beat with electric mixer on high speed until stiff peaks are formed, about 5-7 minutes.

Spread on cake, cookies or crackers.

Ornamental Frosting

My mom and Aunt Hazel always used this frosting to decorate their Christmas cookies. It's very easy to work with and can be stored covered in the refrigerator for five days.

Yield: 2 cups frosting

1/4 cup butter, softened
4 cups powdered sugar
2 egg whites
1 teaspoon vanilla extract
1/4 teaspoon cream of tartar
1-2 teaspoons evaporated milk

In a large bowl, cream butter and sugar with electric mixer on low speed until it resembles cornmeal. Add egg whites, vanilla and cream of tartar. Beat at high speed until thick and smooth, about 5-10 minutes. If frosting becomes too thick, add milk to desired consistency.

White Birthday Cake Frosting

This is an excellent frosting for
Sour Cream Chocolate Cake (page 54).
My mother was a master in transforming the cake
into a masterpiece with this frosting!

Yield: Frosts sides and top
of one 9-inch layer cake

1 cup milk
2 tablespoons cornstarch
1/2 cup (1 stick) butter
1/2 cup shortening
1 cup sugar
1 teaspoon vanilla extract

Combine milk with cornstarch in a small saucepan and cook over low heat until thick, stirring constantly. Remove from heat and allow to cool. (It will become a very stiff custard.)

Cream butter, shortening and sugar in a large bowl; add custard and vanilla. Beat with electric mixer on medium-high speed until light and fluffy and sugar granules are dissolved, about 5-7 minutes. Spread on cooled cake.

Quick Fudge Frosting

*When you are looking for a frosting
you can make in a hurry, this is it!*

Yield: frosts one 13x9-inch cake

1 cup brown sugar, packed
1 square (1 ounce) unsweetened baking
    chocolate, chopped
2 tablespoons shortening
1 tablespoon butter
1/4 teaspoon salt
1/4 cup milk
1 1/2 cups powdered sugar, sifted
1 teaspoon vanilla extract
1/4 cup nuts, chopped

Combine brown sugar, chocolate, shortening, butter, salt and milk in a medium saucepan. Bring mixture to a boil and continue boiling 3 minutes; cool until lukewarm. Stir in powdered sugar, vanilla and nuts.

Spread on cooled cake.

Oatmeal Coconut Cookies

I rushed to the cookie jar to look for these when I came running in from the school bus. They were the best when dunked in a glass of cold milk.

Yield: 5 dozen cookies

1 cup shortening
1 cup brown sugar, packed
2 cups granulated sugar, divided
2 eggs
1 teaspoon vanilla extract
2 cups flour
1 teaspoon baking powder
1 teaspoon baking soda
1 teaspoon salt
1 1/2 cups oatmeal
1 1/2 cups coconut

Preheat oven to 375 degrees. Spray 2 cookie sheets with nonstick cooking spray.

In a large bowl, cream shortening, brown sugar and 1 cup of the granulated sugar with electric mixer on medium speed until light, about 2 minutes. Add eggs and vanilla; mix well.

Sift together flour, baking powder, baking soda and salt; stir into batter. Add oatmeal and coconut; mix until well blended. Shape into 1-inch balls. Roll in remaining 1 cup granulated sugar and place on prepared cookie sheets, 2 inches apart. Bake 10 minutes or until edges are lightly browned. Remove from oven and cool on wire rack.

Sugar Cookies

*This cookie will melt in your mouth.
It makes a large batch so you will be sure
to have plenty on hand.*

Yield: 5-6 dozen cookies

1¹/2 cups granulated sugar, divided
1 cup powdered sugar, sifted
1 cup (2 sticks) butter, softened
1 cup salad oil
2 eggs
1¹/2 teaspoons vanilla extract
4 cups flour
1 teaspoon baking soda
1 teaspoon cream of tartar
1 teaspoon salt
1 cup walnuts, halved

Combine 1 cup of the granulated sugar, powdered sugar, butter and oil in a large bowl. Cream with electric mixer on medium speed until light and fluffy, about 2 minutes. Add eggs and vanilla; beat 1 minute more.

Sift together flour, baking soda, cream of tartar and salt. Gradually stir into creamed mixture until well blended. Cover bowl with plastic wrap and chill in refrigerator several hours.

Preheat oven to 350 degrees. Spray 2 cookie sheets with nonstick cooking spray. Drop dough by teaspoonfuls onto cookie sheets, about 2 inches apart. Place remaining 1/2 cup granulated sugar in a sauce dish; moisten bottom of small glass, dip glass in sugar and flatten each cookie. Place walnut half in center. Bake 10 minutes or until edges are lightly browned. Remove from oven and cool on wire rack.

Chocolate Walnut Kisses

*These cookies are an example of the many kinds
my mom made at Christmas. I usually got the
job of unwrapping all the chocolate kisses
(not all of them made it to the cookies).*

Yield: 3-4 dozen cookies

1 cup (2 sticks) butter, softened
1 1/2 cups powdered sugar, divided
1 teaspoon vanilla extract
2 cups flour
1 cup walnuts or pecans, finely chopped
1 package (5 3/4 ounces) milk chocolate
    kisses, unwrapped

Preheat oven to 375 degrees.

In a medium bowl, cream butter, 1/2 cup of the
powdered sugar and vanilla with electric mixer
on medium speed until fluffy, about 2 minutes.
At low speed, gradually beat in flour and nuts.
Divide dough into 40 equal parts. Shape dough
around chocolate kiss to form a ball; cover
candy completely.

Place on ungreased cookie sheet and bake
12 minutes. Remove from oven and let stand
1 minute. Remove to wire rack and cool slightly,
about 2-3 minutes. Roll each cookie in remaining 1 cup powdered sugar. Store in tightly covered container.

Lessons From My Mom

*A good cook always cleans up
after herself.*

*Don't slam the door—there's a
cake in the oven!*

Ice Box Cookies

*This is another Christmas favorite.
These cookies are especially great because the
dough will keep in the fridge for one week,
and you can bake them as needed.*

Yield: 8-10 dozen cookies

2 cups (4 sticks) butter, softened
1 cup brown sugar, packed
1 cup granulated sugar
1 egg
1 teaspoon vanilla extract
5 cups flour, sifted and divided
1 teaspoon salt
1 teaspoon baking soda
3/4 cup nuts, chopped

When we were growing up we enjoyed the ice box cookie dough as much as the baked cookies. So much so that sometimes Aunt Hazel and my mom would discover the dough missing in the morning. One Christmas, Hazel substituted chicken fat for the butter. Her son Wink raided the ice box that night, proceeded to get very sick and never touched the cookie dough again.

In a large bowl, cream butter, brown sugar and granulated sugar with electric mixer on medium speed until fluffy, about 2 minutes. Add egg and vanilla; mix well. Gradually stir in 4 cups of the flour and salt. Add baking soda to remaining 1 cup flour and stir into mixture. Add nuts and blend well.

Divide dough into 3 equal parts. Shape into logs approximately 2 inches wide by 12 inches long. Wrap in waxed paper and store in refrigerator overnight.

Preheat oven to 375 degrees. Remove dough from refrigerator, 1 log at a time and cut into 1/4-inch slices. Place on ungreased cookie sheet and bake 8-10 minutes or until lightly browned. Remove from oven and cool on wire racks.

Molasses Crinkles

*The aroma of these spices baking will set
your feet moving quickly toward the kitchen.
This is what a good molasses cookie should be—
crispy on the outside and chewy inside.*

Yield: 3 dozen cookies

3/4 cup shortening
1 cup brown sugar
1 egg
4 tablespoons molasses
2 1/4 cups flour
2 teaspoons baking soda
1/2 teaspoon salt
1/2 teaspoon cloves
1 teaspoon cinnamon
1 teaspoon ginger
1/2 cup granulated sugar

In a large bowl, cream shortening and brown sugar with electric mixer on medium speed until light. Add egg and molasses; continue beating until thoroughly blended. Sift together flour, baking soda, salt, cloves, cinnamon and ginger; stir into mixture. Cover bowl with plastic wrap and chill several hours.

Preheat oven to 375 degrees. Spray cookie sheet with nonstick cooking spray. Remove dough from refrigerator. Shape into balls, about walnut size and place on cookie sheet.

Pour granulated sugar in a sauce dish; moisten bottom of small glass, dip glass in sugar and flatten each cookie lightly; bake 10 minutes. (Centers will be slightly soft.) Remove from oven and cool completely on wire racks.

Spritz

*This is a tender, buttery Swedish cookie
that was always baked at Christmas.
The unsalted butter enhances the flavor of this cookie.
A cookie press will be needed for preparation.*

Yield: 6 dozen cookies

1 cup (2 sticks) unsalted butter, softened
2/3 cup sugar
3 egg yolks
3 cups flour, sifted
1/2 cup red and green colored sugars

Preheat oven to 400 degrees.

In a large bowl, cream butter with electric mixer on high speed until light. Add sugar and cream 2 minutes more. Add egg yolks and beat 2 additional minutes. Gradually add flour and stir until completely incorporated. (Dough will become quite stiff.)

Place dough into cookie press and form into desired shape by pressing onto an ungreased cookie sheet. Sprinkle with colored sugars, if desired. Bake 8 minutes or until delicately browned. Remove from oven and cool on wire rack.

In the wintertime the ladies work centered around making hooked rugs and carpet balls for rag rugs. The previous summer was spent scouring rummage sales for any kind of woolen clothing. The neighbor ladies would gather at someone's house, cut the material into strips, sew them together and roll them into balls. There was a lot of hard work, laughter and gossip during those afternoons. Of course, it was always highlighted by coffee and a specially prepared dessert.

The carpet balls would then be brought to a rug maker, and in the spring the ladies would marvel at the finished products. Hooked rugs were also made individually using woolen strips. They were works of art. I wish I had some of those rugs Aunt Hazel and my mom either threw out or sold at their garage sales.

Cut-Out Sugar Cookies

This is the recipe my mom and Aunt Hazel used for their decorated Christmas cookies. My mom displayed so much patience when frosting and decorating her cookies for Christmas.

Yield: 5-6 dozen cookies

  3 cups flour
  1 cup sugar
  1 teaspoon baking soda
$1/2$ teaspoon salt
  1 teaspoon cream of tartar
$11/4$ cups shortening
  3 tablespoons milk
  2 eggs, beaten
  1 teaspoon vanilla extract

Preheat oven to 375 degrees. Prepare cookie sheet by spraying with nonstick cooking spray.

Sift flour, sugar, baking soda, salt and cream of tartar into a large bowl. Cut in shortening with a pastry blender until mixture resembles small peas. Add milk, eggs and vanilla; mix well.

On a floured board, roll dough to $1/8$-inch thickness. Cut with floured cookie cutters; place on prepared sheet. Bake 7-8 minutes or until firm in center. Remove to wire rack and cool.

Note: Ornamental frosting may be used to decorated these cookies.

Bernice made the best Christmas cookies. She took such pains to decorate them just right. Her "wreaths" were everyone's favorite.

—Betty Larson Smiley
(Hazel's daughter)

Bourbon Balls

A traditional Christmas favorite.
It is usually better to make these a few weeks
ahead of time so the flavors have time to mellow.
The more you eat the betttur thay taase!

Yield: 2 dozen bourbon balls

1 cup vanilla wafers
1/2 cup bourbon
11/2 tablespoons white corn syrup
1/2 cup pecans, finely chopped
2 tablespoons cocoa
11/2 cups powdered sugar

Crush wafers in blender at high speed.

Mix bourbon and syrup together in a medium bowl. Add wafer crumbs, pecans and cocoa. Dust hands with powdered sugar and roll dough into small balls, about the size of a walnut. Roll balls in powdered sugar and place on ungreased baking sheet.

Cover with plastic wrap and chill in refrigerator overnight. Store in a tightly covered container.

Aunt Hazel served "flavored" coffees long before they became fashionable. However, her flavors were not Irish Creme, vanilla or mocha; they were Old Crow, Ten High and Aristocrat.

Turtles

*A rich chocolate cookie that is made using a waffle iron.
It's so simple! I usually make a double batch right
away because you rarely get a taste of the first one.
They are so good and really look like turtles.*

Yield: 3 dozen cookies

Cookie:
 2 squares (1 ounce each) unsweetened
    baking chocolate
 1/2 cup (1 stick) butter
 2 eggs, beaten
 3/4 cup sugar
 1 teaspoon vanilla extract
 1 cup flour, sifted

Frosting:
 1/2 square (1/2 ounce) unsweetened baking
    chocolate
 1/2 cup brown sugar, packed
 1/4 cup water
 2 1/2 tablespoons butter
 1 teaspoon vanilla extract
 1 cup powdered sugar (approximate)
 1/4 cup nuts, chopped

Preheat waffle iron to medium-high.

To make cookie, melt chocolate and butter in
a medium saucepan over low heat. Remove
from heat; add eggs, sugar and vanilla. Beat
until well blended; fold in flour. Drop teaspoon
of dough in each corner of waffle iron; bake 80
seconds. Remove to wire rack to cool.

To make frosting, combine chocolate, brown
sugar, water and butter in small saucepan. Bring
to a boil over low heat; continue to boil without
stirring for 3 minutes. Remove from heat and
stir in vanilla. Cool to lukewarm. Stir in powdered sugar to desired consistency. Add nuts.
Spread frosting on cooled cookies.

Filled Cookies

*A plate of these cookies fresh from the oven
will remind you of days gone by. It's a good hearty
cookie to satisfy that big sweet craving.*

Yield: 3 dozen cookies

Filling:
  2 cups dates, chopped
  1/2 cup nuts, chopped
  1 cup sugar
  2 tablespoons flour
  2 tablespoons lemon juice
  1 cup boiling water

Cookie:
  1 cup sugar
  1 cup shortening
  1 egg, slightly beaten
  1 teaspoon vanilla extract
  3 cups flour
  3 teaspoons baking powder
  1/2 teaspoon salt
  1/2 cup milk

Preheat oven to 375 degrees. Spray cookie sheet with nonstick cooking spray.

To make filling, combine dates, nuts, sugar, flour and lemon juice in a small bowl. Stir in boiling water; set aside to cool.

In a large bowl, cream sugar and shortening with electric mixer on medium-high speed until fluffy, about 2 minutes. Add eggs and vanilla; beat 1 minute longer. Sift together flour, baking powder and salt. Add alternately with milk (about 1/3 at a time) to creamed mixture; blend well.

(continued)

Aunt Hazel was notorious for leaving out an ingredient when someone asked for a recipe. Often the recipe recipient would stop at our house on their way home and ask my mom to check it over for "completeness."

Roll dough to 1/4-inch thickness on floured board. Cut dough with floured round cookie cutter and place on prepared sheet. Spoon 1 teaspoon filling in center of each round. Place second round over top. Press edges firmly together. Bake 10 minutes or until delicately browned. Remove from oven and cool on wire rack.

Potato Chip Cookies

*Aunt Hazel loved these cookies.
One summer it seemed this was the only cookie
she baked. The potato chips give the cookie a great
crispiness and a slightly salty flavor.*

Yield: 4 dozen cookies

1 cup (2 sticks) butter, softened
1 1/2 cups powdered sugar, sifted and divided
1 egg yolk
1 teaspoon vanilla extract
1 1/2 cups flour
1/2 teaspoon baking soda
1/2 cup nuts, chopped
1 cup potato chips, crushed

Preheat oven to 350 degrees.

In a large bowl, cream butter and 1 cup of the powdered sugar with electric mixer on medium speed until light and fluffy, about 2 minutes. Add egg yolk and vanilla; beat well. Sift flour and baking soda together; fold into mixture. Stir in nuts and potato chips.

Place by teaspoonfuls onto an ungreased cookie sheet. Bake 10 minutes or until edges are lightly browned. Remove to waxed paper and sprinkle with remaining powdered sugar while still warm. Cool on wire rack.

Jan and Tom Bahr, who have a summer home in Appleport, found a solution for the missing ingredient which Hazel conveniently omitted from her recipes. They would wait until they got back to Chicago and then call Hazel and ask her to repeat the recipe. They discovered that Hazel sometimes forgot which ingredient she had omitted from the first request.

Brownies

The marshmallows between the brownie and frosting really make these outstanding.

Yield: one 9-inch pan

Brownie:
    1/2 cup (1 stick) butter
    2 squares (1 ounce each) unsweetened
        baking chocolate
    2 eggs, beaten
    1 cup sugar
    1 teaspoon vanilla extract
    3/4 cup flour
    1/2 teaspoon baking powder
    1/2 teaspoon salt
    1/2 cup nuts, chopped
    25 large marshmallows

Frosting:
    2 tablespoons butter, softened
    2 squares (1 ounce each) unsweetened
        baking chocolate, melted
    1 teaspoon vanilla extract
    1/2 teaspoon salt
    2 cups powdered sugar

Preheat oven to 350 degrees. Spray a 9x9-inch cake pan with nonstick cooking spray.

Melt butter and chocolate in a medium saucepan over low heat. Remove from heat and add eggs. Stir in sugar and vanilla. Sift together flour, baking powder and salt in a small bowl. Add to chocolate mixture and blend well; add nuts. Spread into prepared pan. Bake 25 minutes or until wooden pick inserted in center comes out clean. Remove from oven and place marshmallows on top. Return to oven and bake an additional 5 minutes.

(continued)

To prepare frosting, combine butter, chocolate, vanilla and salt in a medium bowl. Stir in powdered sugar to desired consistency. Remove brownies from oven and gently spread marshmallows evenly over top. Carefully cover marshmallows with frosting.

Melting Moments

*A delicate, tender cookie
perfect for afternoon coffee or tea.*

Yield: 2 dozen cookies

Cookie:
- 3/4 cup butter
- 1/4 cup powdered sugar
- 1 teaspoon vanilla extract
- 2 cups flour, sifted

Frosting:
- 1 cup powdered sugar
- 1 tablespoon butter, softened
- 1-2 teaspoons milk

In a medium bowl, beat butter, sugar and vanilla with electric mixer on medium speed until creamy, about 2 minutes. Add flour and stir until well blended. Shape dough into 2 rolls. Wrap in waxed paper and chill several hours in refrigerator.

Preheat oven to 350 degrees. Cut rolls into 1/8-inch-thick slices. Place on ungreased cookie sheet and bake 10 minutes or until light brown. Remove from oven and cool on wire rack.

To prepare frosting, combine sugar and butter in a small bowl. Add milk to desired consistency. Food coloring may be added to frosting to make cookies more decorative. Spread frosting on two cookies at a time and press together to make a "sandwich."

Krumkake

A "krumkake iron" is required to make this special Swedish cookie. You can easily spot these cone-shaped, delicate treats on a cookie plate—they melt in your mouth!

Yield: 3 dozen krumkake

4 eggs
1 cup sugar
1 teaspoon vanilla extract
1/2 cup (1 stick) butter, melted, cooled
1 cup flour
1/4 cup cornstarch

In a large bowl, beat eggs, sugar and vanilla with electric mixer on medium-high speed until thick, about 10 minutes. Fold in butter. Sift flour and cornstarch together and add to batter. Cover bowl with plastic wrap and chill 1 hour.

To bake, preheat krumkake iron over medium-high heat. Place a drop of water on iron; if it dances around, your iron is ready. Drop a rounded teaspoon of batter on center of iron. Close lid quickly and bake until slightly browned around edges, about 60-80 seconds. Remove from iron using a spatula or table knife and place on cutting board. While still hot, quickly roll into a cone shape. Allow to cool. (They will become quite crisp.) Store in a tightly covered tin.

Occasionally my dad would say to my mom, "You're just like your mother," and it wasn't always said in a complimentary manner. But she took it as praise "because I like my mom."

Rosettes

A special tool called a rosette iron is needed to make these cookies. A good Swedish baker always includes rosettes as a specialty.

Yield: 2 dozen rosettes

    2 eggs
    1 egg yolk
  1/3 cup sugar
  1/4 teaspoon salt
    1 cup flour, sifted
  2/3 cup heavy cream
  1/4 teaspoon vanilla extract
  2-3 cups cooking oil
    1 cup powdered sugar

In a medium bowl, beat eggs and yolk with electric mixer on medium speed, about 2 minutes. Blend in sugar and salt. Stir in flour (about 1/3 at a time) alternately with cream; add vanilla.

Heat 3-4 inches oil in a medium saucepan to fry stage or 185 degrees on a candy thermometer. Place iron in hot oil; dip into batter. (Be careful not to let batter go over top of iron.) Place iron in oil and fry until golden brown, about 1-2 minutes. As it is frying, carefully remove rosette from iron with fork. Remove from pan and place on paper towel to cool.

When cool, sprinkle lightly with powdered sugar. Store tightly covered in a metal tin.

Fattigman

Fattigman have a doughnut-like texture and are truly a Scandinavian favorite. Aunt Hazel taught me how to make these one Christmas when I was a teenager. We really got into the holiday spirit and decided to tint them red and green. We only tried that once!

Yield: 3-4 dozen fattigman

1/2 cup (1 stick) butter
3/4 cup sugar
3 eggs
2 tablespoons cream
2 tablespoons whiskey
1/2 teaspoon baking powder
3 cups flour
3-4 cups cooking oil

In a large bowl, beat butter and sugar with electric mixer on medium speed, about 2 minutes. Add eggs, cream and whiskey; beat 2 minutes more. Sift baking powder and flour together; add to mixture.

On a floured board, roll dough to 1/8-inch thickness. Cut into 2x4-inch pieces. Make a 2-inch lengthwise slit in each piece and twist one end through slit. Set on waxed paper until ready to fry.

Heat oil in a medium saucepan to fry stage or 185 degrees on a candy thermometer. Fry 3 or 4 at a time (turning over halfway through) until golden brown, about 2-3 minutes. Remove to paper towel to cool. Store in a covered metal container.

Winter's Night Fudge

A cold winter's night seemed the perfect time to stir up a batch of fudge. Aunt Hazel's children, Betty and Wink, often walked down the hill to our house and asked my mom to do just that.

Yield: 2 1/2 dozen pieces

2 squares (1 ounce each) unsweetened
    baking chocolate
2 cups sugar
3/4 cup milk
2 tablespoons corn syrup
1/8 teaspoon salt
2 tablespoons butter
1/2 teaspoon vanilla extract
1/2 cup nuts, chopped (optional)

Butter a 9-inch square pan.

Melt chocolate over low heat in a medium saucepan. Blend sugar into melted chocolate. Stir in milk, corn syrup and salt. Place over low heat and stir until sugar is dissolved. Quit stirring when mixture begins to boil. Boil until soft ball forms when tested in cold water or temperature reaches 234 degrees on a candy thermometer.

Remove from heat and drop in butter; do not stir. Cool until hand can be placed on bottom of pan. Beat with spoon until creamy and slightly dull in appearance. Add vanilla and nuts. Pour into prepared pan and allow to cool.

Secrets for making candy:

1. *Assemble all ingredients and utensils.*
2. *Mix together sugar and other dry ingredients.*
3. *Add liquid and mix well.*
4. *Place over a low flame.*
5. *Stir until mixture is clear and sugar is dissolved.*
6. *Never stir while mixture is boiling.*
7. *Do not let mixture start to boil until sugar is dissolved.*
8. *Test often in cold water.*
9. *When soft ball stage is reached, remove from fire at once.*
10. *Place in a pan of cold water.*
11. *Drop in butter (do not stir).*
12. *Let stand in cold water until cool.*
13. *Beat until smooth, creamy and a little dull in appearance.*
14. *Stir in vanilla and nuts.*
15. *Pour at once onto waxed paper.*

—From my mom's
home economics class at
Denfeld High School,
Duluth, Minnesota,
(about 1939).

Popcorn Balls

We had great fun making popcorn balls. Usually it was a Halloween treat, but they are great any time of year.

Yield: 20-24 popcorn balls

6 quarts popped corn
2 cups sugar
2/3 cup corn syrup
2/3 cup water
1/2 cup (1 stick) butter
1 1/2 teaspoons salt
1 1/2 teaspoons vanilla extract

Place popped corn in a large roasting pan.

Combine sugar, corn syrup, water, butter and salt in a large saucepan. Bring to a boil and continue boiling until syrup reaches hard ball stage or 250 degrees on a candy thermometer. Stir in vanilla and immediately pour over popped corn; mix well. Moisten hands with butter and work quickly to form into balls.

Set balls on waxed paper to cool. When cool, wrap individually in a baggie or plastic wrap.

Canning
and Pickling

Canning and Pickling

Why We Will Miss Her

from the Door County Advocate—
October 1995

I had to write. I have written before about taxes and moving the library from the park in Sister Bay. But this time writing is difficult. Door County and Sister Bay have lost something special and wonderful: a very special lady, Hazel Larson. The problem is, how do you describe a person who takes you in and makes you part of her life without question? That was Hazel, and that is why we will miss her.

Hazel was more, much more. A stop by the house was required each time we came up. "Coffee" at the kitchen table was not an option. If you just couldn't stop, you honked to let her know you were up, and honked "goodbye" as you left.

I'm sure you all know that Hazel is gone. I just had to let you know that she touched our lives and how we felt. To Betty, Audrey, Richard and the rest of the family, we will miss her almost as much as you. And we will always honk as we go by the house.

—Frank Tarpey
(a regular at
Hazel's kitchen table)
Highland Park, Illinois

Hazel's Famous Dill Pickles

Aunt Hazel didn't make these pickles for herself. She worked at a frantic pace to line up the shelves of her cellar with 50–75 quarts of these pickles each fall. She begged cucumbers from everyone. When she left for warmer parts each winter, one by one these jars made their way out of her unlocked cellar, so by spring it looked pretty empty. Her family and many friends appreciated the fruits of her labor more than she knew.

Yield: 8 quarts

25-30	medium cucumbers
2	bunches dill
3	cloves garlic, sliced
2	quarts water
2	quarts vinegar
3	cups sugar
1	cup canning salt

Sterilize eight 1-quart canning jars.

Wash and dry cucumbers. Slice in half lengthwise. Place a layer of dill in bottom of each jar. Pack in cucumbers. Add layer of dill and 2-3 slices of garlic on top.

To make brine, boil water, vinegar, sugar and salt in a large kettle for 2 minutes. Pour brine over pickles. Seal jars immediately and store in a cool place.

Sliced Cucumber Pickles

*There seems to be an infinite variety of pickles.
These have a touch of sweetness when
combined with the spices.*

Yield: 8 pints

30 small cucumbers
 1 quart small onions
 1 cup canning salt
 1 gallon water
 1 quart vinegar
 2 teaspoons celery seed
 2 teaspoons cinnamon
 2 cups sugar
 2 teaspoons dry mustard
1/2 teaspoon cayenne pepper

Sterilize eight 1-pint canning jars.

Wash cucumbers. Slice cucumbers and onions
and place in a large bowl. Cover with salt and
water. Let stand overnight; drain.

Boil vinegar, celery seed, cinnamon, sugar,
mustard and cayenne in a large kettle. Add
cucumbers and onions. Simmer 20 minutes.
Pack in hot jars and seal.

Celery Pickles

My mom and Aunt Hazel made many different varieties of pickles. Winters could get pretty long, and it was always special to open a new jar of pickles at a meal.

Yield: 4 quarts

25 medium cucumbers
 1 bunch celery
 2 medium onions, sliced thick
 1 quart water
 1 quart vinegar
 2 cups sugar
1/2 canning salt

Sterilize four 1-quart canning jars.

Wash and dry cucumbers. Cut into quarters. Cut celery same length as cucumbers. Pack cucumbers into jars. Slip celery in spaces between cucumbers. Lay slice of onion on top.

In a large kettle, boil water, vinegar, sugar and salt until clear, about 15 minutes. Pour over cucumbers and seal.

Bread-and-Butter Pickles

This pickle was a staple among devout pickle makers. Jars of these pickles in the cellar surrounded by all the other varieties were the sign of a household that took great pride in taking care of their family.

Yield: 8 pints

1 gallon medium cucumbers
8 medium white onions, sliced
1/2 cup canning salt
5 cups sugar
5 cups vinegar
1 tablespoon mustard seed
1 teaspoon celery seed
1 teaspoon turmeric

Sterilize eight 1-pint canning jars.

Wash and dry cucumbers. Cut into 1/4-inch slices. Combine cucumbers and onions in a large bowl. Sprinkle with salt; let stand 3 hours. Rinse with cold water; drain.

In a large kettle, combine sugar, vinegar, mustard seed, celery seed and turmeric. Boil 10 minutes. Add cucumbers and onions. Return to boil; remove from heat immediately. Pack in hot jars and seal.

One time during the summer Hazel was making some head cheese. She had gone to someone in Ellison Bay and gotten a whole pig's head and was cooking it in a huge pressure cooker. For some unknown reason the cooker exploded and blew the lid into the kitchen ceiling. The steam scalded both her hands, and we had to drive her to the hospital in Sturgeon Bay with her hands in a pail of water. It must have been terribly painful, but I remember her going about her business of cooking and taking care of the house days later with her hands and arms wrapped in gauze bandages.

—Betty Larson Smiley
(Hazel's daughter)

Green Tomato Pickles

*When you are getting impatient for those tomatoes
to ripen, try picking the green ones.
They make a great pickle!*

Yield: 3 quarts

25-30 medium green tomatoes
1/2 cup canning salt
3 cups vinegar
7 cups sugar
3 teaspoons whole allspice
1 teaspoon mustard seed
1 teaspoon celery seed

Sterilize three 1-quart canning jars.

Slice tomatoes. Combine tomatoes and salt in a large pan. Cover with water and let stand overnight; drain.

Combine vinegar and sugar in a large kettle. Tie allspice, mustard seed and celery seed in a cheesecloth bag. Add to kettle; boil 5 minutes. Cool slightly; add tomatoes and simmer 30 minutes. Pack in hot jars and seal.

*Land, the only thing they aren't
making any more of.*

—Wink's motto (Hazel's son)

Ripe Cucumber Relish

Relishes are an excellent accompaniment to roasts and poultry. They are even better when the ingredients are fresh from your own garden.

Yield: 8 pints

12 large ripe cucumbers
 1 cup canning salt
 1 cup water
 4 cups vinegar
 5 cups sugar
 3 tablespoons mustard seed
 3 tablespoons celery seed
 1 bunch celery, cut up
 3 red peppers, cut up
 3 green peppers, cut up
 2 large onions, cut up

Sterilize eight 1-pint canning jars.

Peel cucumbers and remove seeds; place in a large bowl. Add salt and cover with water. Let stand overnight. Drain and coarsely chop cucumbers.

Bring water, vinegar, sugar, mustard seed and celery seed to a boil in a large kettle. Add cucumbers, celery, red peppers, green peppers and onion. Boil until cucumbers are clear, but not soft, about 15 minutes. Pack in hot jars and seal.

Mustard Pickles

This recipe is a combination of a pickle and a relish. If you don't have a garden, a trip to the farmers' market or a roadside stand should provide you with all the produce you will need.

Yield: 4 quarts

1 quart large cucumbers, cubed
1 quart small whole cucumbers
1 quart onions, thinly sliced
1 quart green tomatoes, coarsely chopped
2 red peppers, finely chopped
1 large cauliflower, broken into
    small flowerets
1/2 cup canning salt
1 quart water
2 cups sugar
6 tablespoons dry mustard
1 tablespoon turmeric
1 cup flour
2 quarts vinegar

Sterilize four 1-quart canning jars.

Place cucumbers, onion, green tomatoes, peppers and cauliflower in a large kettle. Cover with salt and water. Let stand 24 hours. Bring vegetable mixture to boil in same solution. Remove from heat and drain.

Mix sugar, mustard, turmeric, flour and vinegar in same kettle. Cook until thick, about 10 minutes. Stir in vegetables. Heat thoroughly. Pack in hot jars and seal.

When my dad, Emery Larson, began bowling at the Sister Bay Bowl, he was well into his 40s. He grew to love the game with a passion and bowled whenever he got the chance. His diligence was rewarded in December of 1963 when he bowled a perfect "300" game. It was the first ever at "The Bowl" and second in Door County history, so it received a lot of attention and publicity. He also received a beautiful gold watch for his accomplishment. In an attempt to bring my dad back down to earth, Al Johnson chided, "For all the money you paid to get that game, all you got was a watch! Hell, I could have given you a watch."

Refrigerator Pickles

The recipe is simple, the pickles are stored right in your refrigerator and the crispness lasts for about 3 months. What could be better than that?

Yield: 6 pints

  8 cups cucumbers, sliced thin
1/2 cup canning salt
  1 medium onion, sliced thin
  1 small green pepper, sliced thin
  1 small red pepper, sliced thin
  4 cups sugar
  4 cups vinegar
11/2 teaspoons celery seed
11/2 teaspoons mustard seed
  1 teaspoon turmeric

Sterilize six 1-pint canning jars.

In a large bowl, combine cucumbers, salt, onion and peppers. Cover with water and let stand overnight; drain.

Combine sugar, vinegar, celery seed, mustard seed and turmeric in another large bowl. Stir until sugar is dissolved. Pour over cucumber mixture; mix well. Pack mixture in jars and seal. Store in refrigerator; keeps for 3 months.

Watermelon Pickles

As kids, these pickles were a real sweet treat.
It's hard to imagine such a delicacy can be made
from watermelon rind.

Yield: 4 pints

3 pounds watermelon rind
4 1/2 quarts water, divided
1/2 cup canning salt
2 pounds sugar
2 cups white vinegar
6 cinnamon sticks (3-inch)
2 tablespoons whole allspice
2 tablespoons whole cloves

Sterilize four 1-pint canning jars.

Pare green skin from rind and remove any pink portions. Cut rind into 2x1-inch pieces and place in a large bowl. Add salt and 2 quarts of the water; let stand 24 hours. Drain.

Place rind in a large kettle; add 2 more quarts of the water and cook until tender, about 10 minutes; drain. Combine remaining 1/2 quart water, sugar and vinegar in same kettle. Boil 5 minutes. Pack watermelon rind in hot jars. Add cinnamon stick, a few pieces of allspice and 2 of the cloves. Pour boiling syrup over rind and seal.

Process jars in hot water bath until rind is transparent, about 30-45 minutes.

Slippery Jims

An excellent way to make use of those overripe cucumbers.

Yield: 6 pints

8-10 large ripe yellow cucumbers
  1 cup canning salt
  2 quarts water
  3 tablespoons alum
  7 cups sugar
  1 quart white vinegar
  1 cup water
  1 tablespoon whole cloves
  1 ounce stick cinnamon

Sterilize six 1-pint canning jars.

Pare and slice cucumbers lengthwise. Remove seeds and cut into 1x3-inch pieces. Place cucumbers and salt in a large bowl and cover with water. Let stand overnight. Drain; return cucumbers to bowl. Boil water with alum in a large saucepan. Pour over cucumbers and let stand 1 hour. Drain and chill cucumbers in ice cold water.

Prepare syrup by combining sugar, vinegar and water in a large kettle. Tie cloves and cinnamon in a cheesecloth bag and add to kettle; boil 3 minutes. Add cucumbers and simmer until liquid is clear, about 10 minutes. Pack in hot jars and seal.

I remember my aunts coming from Chicago to stay for weeks in the summertime. They would can peaches, pears and cherries. They all wore aprons. I can still see them sitting at the kitchen table with aprons full of string beans and snapping them as they visited. I remember the rows of lovely, shiny quart jars resting on the stove after a day of canning.

—Betty Larson Smiley
(Hazel's daughter)

Pickled Beets

Pickled Beets may not be as fashionable today,
but they were a must to can when I was growing up.
Their rich red color and sweetness add
a touch of class to any dinner.

Yield: 4 pints

4 pounds beets
1 stick cinnamon
1 tablespoon whole allspice
2 cups sugar
2 1/2 cups vinegar
2 1/2 cups beet water

Sterilize four 1-pint canning jars.

Wash beets. Cook beets in a large kettle of boiling water until tender, about 10 minutes. Drain, reserving water. Remove skins, roots and tops; cut into 1/8-inch-thick slices. Tie cinnamon and allspice in a cheesecloth bag.

Heat sugar, vinegar, reserved beet water and spice bag in same kettle to boiling. Add beets and continue boiling 5 minutes. Remove spice bag; pack beets into hot jars. Fill jars with liquid and seal.

Pickled Peaches

*These can be served at any meal,
or they are great right out of the jar.
There was always a great variety
of home-canned fruit on hand.*

Yield: 4 quarts

4 quarts whole peaches
6 cups sugar, divided
2 cups water
3 cups vinegar
2 sticks cinnamon
1 tablespoon whole allspice
1 tablespoon whole cloves

Sterilize four 1-quart canning jars.

Wash and dry peaches. Combine 2 cups of the sugar, water and vinegar in a large kettle. Tie cinnamon, allspice and cloves in a cheesecloth bag; add to mixture. Boil 3 minutes. Add 10-12 peaches at a time and simmer until tender, about 10 minutes. Continue until all peaches are used. Let stand in syrup 24 hours. Add 2 more cups of the sugar and return mixture to boil again. Let stand 24 hours in syrup.

Add remaining 2 cups sugar; boil until sugar is dissolved. Pack in hot jars and seal. Immerse jars in hot water bath for 10 minutes to complete seal.

There's no doubt about it—Aunt Hazel had a lot of wrinkles. She blamed them on a banana diet she tried years ago. They were the source of many good-natured jokes and definitely contributed to her "character."

Memories

Appleport and the Larsons

Appleport is located east of Sister Bay in Door County, Wisconsin. It is situated east of Old Stage Road to Lake Michigan and between Sand Bay and Marshall's Point. However these boundaries are informal, and you will not find it on any map or road sign—and its residents prefer it that way.

Appleport was settled in the mid 1800s as a lakeside port primarily used by loggers. Due to the shallow water, a 400- to 500-foot pier was constructed, and the logs were taken by raft to ships waiting offshore. This "industry" was short-lived however; most of the trees were harvested, and the need to ship logs from this location was eliminated.

Emptying the pond nets.

My grandparents, John and Anna Larson, settled in Appleport around 1900 and purchased the pier and the home next to it. They tried farming for a time but eventually settled on commercial fishing. Another dock was built at the end of Appleport Lane and business was bustling. Fish shanties were constructed along the shoreline. Herring was the primary catch, although there were some perch and whitefish. Pond nets, which were nets strung on long posts that had been driven into the lake bottom, were set from the boat in the very early morning. Later in the afternoon the nets would be lifted from the poles and the day's catch would be spilled into the hull of the boat. It was easy to tell if it was a good catch by the number of sea gulls hovering over the boat as it chugged back to shore.

In 1947 my dad Emery and his brother Everett (Hazel's husband) built the last dock several hundred feet down from their father's home. They carried on the family fishing tradition until the mid 1950s when the herring population in Lake Michigan became scarce.

In the late 1920s, my grandfather also ventured into the cherry business. It seemed the cherry trees thrived in the rocky limestone soil. Sometimes dynamite had to be used to create a hole in the rocks to plant trees. So, as they had followed in their father's footsteps in the fishing business, they now turned their attention to cherries. Eventually Everett and Hazel had their own orchard, as did my mom and dad. Migrants were recruited to handpick the cherries and were housed in the old fish shanties that had been moved up from the lakeshore. Each shack had two beds, a table and chair, a two-burner stove and an ice box. Blocks of ice were taken from the lake in the dead of winter and stored in sawdust. These blocks became a water source and ice box supply. The migrants were always treated with respect and many became special friends. Hazel and my mom always hosted a picnic at the end of the season.

Everett's death in 1956 and my dad becoming involved in his own business led to the abandonment of the orchards in the early 1960s. Even though picking cherries was probably my least favorite thing to do, the days spent in the orchard and the camaraderie are some of my fondest memories.

If Appleport could talk, it would have many tales to tell. It saw the passing of logging, commercial fishing and cherry orchards. But most importantly, it retains the memories of the lives of many hard-working, loving families. The fish shanties and cherry trees are transitory, but the memories live on forever.

Appleport fish shanties.

A Christmas Reverie

Christmas is here; the bells are clanging on the frosty air; the keen wind whistles about the house. I pull down the curtains against the early darkness that settles on the world and give myself over to my own selfish comfort, forgetting all else. Surely on one night in the year one may forget that there is want and hunger and suffering in the world; surely on one evening one may give himself up to memory. I draw the curtain more closely, settle back in my easy chair and watch the coal fire throw its steady light against the wall.

How quickly the mind travels—faster even than the swiftest reindeer of which children are told on nights like this. I shut my eyes and I am back to Christmas on the farm—on the old homestead. I am with the older ones getting the tree—tramping through the deep snow to find a "real one" with the branches just so; I hear the hack of the axe, the echo in the woods and see the ice and snow shiver on the branches and fall in a shower of crystal. I help them drag the green thing home in the snow along the streamlet that ran like a strand of silver around the hill, our red faces stung by the fierce north wind; I help them shake the flaky whiteness from the balsam and bring it inside to the admiration and glee of the youngsters; and my nostrils catch again the scent of the good things that were ours at Christmas time; I help them trim the green boughs with the bright things and the cookies loaded with colored sugar. And when it is all done we wait for all the folks to come in before the tree is lit; and then I join with the other youngsters in the riot of song and the tumult of mirth while the candlelight blazes and while the older ones sit back in sober happiness, watching the fun, thinking of other days as I am thinking now; and then the expected one has come and the door is flung wide open for the wanderer's return—and all the brood is home and happy at this Christmas time. How they are scattered now, and some come not again though many a Christmas pass, no matter how wide may be for them the door of heart and home, but yet they seem more near this Christmas Eve when memory reaches back, and the lost years for a brief time are ours again.

I see the presents handed 'round—the joy on the youngsters' faces at the gifts the dear, good Santa has brought them; I see the greater joy upon the faces of the givers; ah! they are the real Santas that will keep Christmas always in the world though fables grow old and locks grow gray.

And when the hour is late, the tumult grows quiet and each finds a place to store his treasures until the morn that cannot come too soon, and finally convinced that it is bedtime even on Christmas Eve, they rub their eyes and creep upstairs to dream of good little elves and tinkling bells outside in the blustery dark, while the frost creaks in the rafters over their warm beds. The house is still, but the one who falls last asleep can hear the good Saint Nicholas stuffing the stockings that hang in a row upon the chimney or the noise of someone making shavings for the morning fire. And then a grown-up kid goes to bed and fancies he can hear the rush of swift reindeer through the night and the tread of Santa Claus' feet in the soft whiteness outside.

Bennett Larson (author's great-uncle)
—from his book *A Slender Sheaf*, published in 1947

Night Wind

The wind is at my window and the dark skies wildly weep,
And I, turning on my pillow, hear dim voices through my sleep
And it seems as though they tell me, "We will never come again,"
In the sighing of the wind and the sobbing of the rain.

And my mind roams with the night wind, brooding where the wet grass waves,
By the leafless branches, moaning loud about their early graves;
But I hear far voices whisper, "We are resting without pain,"
In the sighing of the wind and the sobbing of the rain.

And I know the wind will tire and I know the storm will end,
memory take the place of grieving for the absent friend,
And the mind is soothed with slumber and the heart is glad again,
In the sighing of the wind and the sobbing of the rain;
In the crying of the wind and the weeping of the rain.

Bennett Larson (author's great-uncle)
—from his book *A Slender Sheaf*, published in 1947

Index

Index

Index